JB JOSSEY-BASS™
A Wiley Brand

T0342381

How to Plan a Profitable, Wow-factor Gala

Scott C. Stevenson, Editor

WILEY

How to Plan Profitable, WOW-factor Galas

Published by

Stevenson, Inc.

P.O. Box 4528 • Sioux City, Iowa • 51104

Phone 712.239.3010 • Fax 712.239.2166

www.stevensoninc.com

How to Plan Profitable, WOW-Factor Galas

Table of Contents

How to Plan Profitable, WOW-Factor Galas

ESSENTIAL FIRST STEPS

To plan a gala that people will talk about for weeks to come and raise more money than you dreamed possible, lots of up front planning is critical. It's equally important that you begin the planning process by addressing some key questions, even if it's an annual event. These first steps will put your gala on firm footing and everyone involved will have a collective vision for what needs to happen and when.

Checklists Guide You Through Planning a Gala

Content not available in this edition

Before deciding on a special event and becoming immersed in details surrounding it, look at the big picture first. Use a checklist filled with items such as these to decide in advance what your event is intended to accomplish and the audience you intend to attract:

- ❑ What is the event's primary purpose?
- ❑ Who/how many will you attract?
- ❑ What is the price to attend?
- ❑ Where/when will the event be held?
- ❑ Will this event compete with others?
- ❑ How much revenue will it generate?
- ❑ What will be your revenue sources?
- ❑ What costs will you incur and how will they be covered?
- ❑ What time of day will the event take place, and how long will it last?
- ❑ How much planning time is needed?
- ❑ How will you attract attendees?
- ❑ Will sponsors be sought to underwrite costs?
- ❑ How many volunteers will be required and what roles will they play?
- ❑ Who can assume leadership for overseeing the event?

To help you plan and maximize your event's success, start with a simple initial planning checklist and then follow up with a detailed plan. Use these examples to create ones that fit your organization's specific needs.

Content not available in this edition

10 Dos and Don'ts of Event Planning

Experienced event planners have seen it all. Why not learn from that experience when planning your next nonprofit event?

Jodi Bos, principal of In Any Event by Jodi Bos, LLC (Grand Rapids, MI), has 16 years experience as an event planner, including six years working in the nonprofit sector. Here, Bos offers her most valuable dos and don'ts for event planning:

1. **Don't restrict your creativity because you have a limited budget.** There are so many ways to make an event look spectacular, even on a limited budget. For example, instead of using just one specialty linen in the room, mix three coordinating linens. You'll get powerful impact, and it won't cost you anything extra.

2. **Do consider signature drinks.** One hot trend in the event planning industry is offering signature drinks during cocktail hour. Adopt this trend at your next fundraiser. Not only is it creative, it's also cost-effective. Guests won't even miss that full bar, because they'll be so thrilled with the creative concoctions you're offering.

3. **Don't skimp when it comes to centerpieces.** Budget enough money for a substantial centerpiece. Pay attention to scale when creating a beautiful table. If you can't allocate additional funds to centerpieces, consider an alternative such as displaying the dessert in the center of the table and encouraging guests to serve themselves.

4. **Do get crafty and embrace your local thrift store.** For a recent fundraiser produced with a limited budget, Bos scoured local thrift stores for brass candlesticks, acquiring more than 200. Bos and her staff cleaned and spray painted them with enamel paint, added white taper candles and clustered the candlesticks in groups on the tables, making the room glow in candlelight and setting the perfect mood.

5. **Don't be afraid to mix table shapes and sizes when designing your room layout.** There's nothing more boring than a room full of round tables! Mix it up and don't be afraid to fill a room with a combination of round, square and rectangular tables.

6. **Do think outside the box when selecting the time of your event.** Breakfast and lunch events are incredibly cost-effective. You might be surprised to find that more people attend your fundraiser when it isn't scheduled during evening hours.

7. **Do browse event planning magazines and websites.** Adapt ideas to your event.

8. **Don't be afraid of color and texture.** Take your cues from fashion and create event décor using the principles of color and texture that you see in fashion. Gone are the days where an event is decorated in just red, for example. Now, you'll see red paired with aqua and accented with black.

9. **Do check Craigslist (www.craigslist.com) often.** You'll be amazed at what people sell there. You'll find brides selling all of their leftover wedding décor like apothecary jars, glass vases used for centerpieces and candles. You can snap these treasures up for pennies on the dollar and put them to good use at your next event.

10. **Don't be afraid to try something unique when it comes to food.** Offer food stations where guests roam around a room and mingle while eating or serving dinner family style where guests pass serving dishes around the table. These ideas promote guest interaction and facilitate a more creative and memorable event.

Source: Jodi Bos, Principal, In Any Event by Jodi Bos, LLC, Grand Rapids, MI.
E-mail: info@in-any-event.org

Identify Your Event's Intended Audience

In planning a special event, it's critical that you determine just whom it is you intend to have as attendees. Without knowing that, you might come up with an event that appeals to no one.

Potential audiences may include, but not be limited to:

- The general public.
- Repeat supporters.
- Corporate guests.
- Small emerging groups.
- A captive audience.

Knowing the characteristics of expected attendees will drive key planning decisions:

- Ticket price.
- Venue, food and decorations.
- Theme, level of formality.
- Entertainment.
- Methods of promotion.
- Items for sale.

Learn to Spot, Establish Procedures for Gala Crowd

Special events are a great opportunity to introduce your organization to potential donors and supporters. Yet the savvy fundraiser knows that some individuals simply want to see and be seen at a trendy event. Interested primarily in social interaction in a beautiful setting, members of this group are sometimes referred to as the gala crowd.

There is nothing wrong with the gala crowd. They can be engaged, cultivated, even solicited. But nonprofits should also develop a procedure for determining when sufficient outreach has been attempted, and the gala-goer will be categorized as a special events ticket buyer and nothing more.

Cue-to-cue List Helps Anticipate Every Aspect

In planning any type of event, the cue-to-cue as it's often called — your schedule of events that outlines what happens when, who does what and where everything takes place — should address every detail of your event: setup information, guest arrival, transportation, food deliveries and pickups, venue information, cleanup and more.

Everything that will happen before, during and immediately following the day of the event should be included in the cue-to-cue. The more information you can include, the better informed everyone will be and the more smoothly the event will flow.

To develop a cue-to-cue, walk through every aspect of your event from start to finish with all the key people involved in the planning. Put yourself in the shoes of a participant, asking these and other key questions: What do I see? Where do I go? How do I get there? What does it look like? Now think about all the factors and event elements that go into making that experience happen.

Developing a cue-to-cue is an ongoing process. You should expect to go through many drafts as you change and update this important tool several times prior to your special event.

Once the final cue-to-cue is developed, review and share the document with each of your key people.

Maximizing Ticket Revenue — Price or Volume?

 "When it comes to fundraising events, which will net you more overall revenue, a higher-priced ticket with fewer attendees or an inexpensive ticket price with far more guests attending?"

"Based on recent experience, I feel an event with a higher-priced ticket will net more overall revenue. A little over 18 months ago, the Clay Center's volunteer fundraising group Friends evaluated our fundraising events lineup. Based on trends we were seeing, and changes in income experienced at these events, we decided to move from several events with inexpensive ticket prices ($25-50/person) to a larger event with a higher admission ($125-150/person). The new event attracted a large audience because we were able to focus more marketing resources, and secure greater sponsorship income, and had the whole town talking about the fundraiser. This single event achieved a net income in excess of the overall net fundraising from the past event line-up."

— *Missy Menefee, Membership & Special Events Manager, Clay Center (Charleston, WV)*

"I believe the goal of the event guides you to choose high cost/low attendance or low cost/high attendance. When the event is community- or publicity-based, the goal is to spread the word about your agency to as many people as possible. This goal is best accomplished with a large number of guests. Activities like egg hunts, dances, trivia nights and concerts-for-the-cause are good for this publicity-based goal. A goal of the high dollar/low attendance event is to host an event for those looking to support and/or participate in an event which is thought of as exclusive or the guest is considered a distinctive donor. I believe it is best to host both types of events for guests/supporters to gain a higher level/range of community support."

— *Kathy Wilson, Event Coordinator, Hospice of Southern Illinois (Belleville, IL)*

"Each event needs to be analyzed individually. You need to look at your target audience, whether it's families or adults only. Attendees need to feel like they are getting a good value for their money. For an event such as a walk-a-thon you want a bigger audience to make it more worthwhile, so the entry fee is less expensive, but for an adult-only or specialized event where attendance is not a driving factor, a higher ticket price and solid sponsorship strategy are the keys to a successful event."

— *Sherris Johnson, Director of Special Events, Ivy Tech Community College (Indianapolis, IN)*

Use Venue Selection to Weave the Wow Factor Into Your Event

Venue selection is critical to the success of any event, says Stacey Hoyt, owner of the event planning and consulting firm, Stacey Hoyt Events (Austin, TX). "Not only does the location affect the ambiance and flow of an event," Hoyt says, "but the venue selection can also have a huge impact on the event's bottom line."

The professional event planner addresses elements in finding a location with the wow factor that will win over guests:

Aim for a Blank Slate

To create an event unlike any other, a nontraditional or blank slate venue may be what you are looking for, Hoyt says. Think of a venue with nondescript architecture that would be a neutral backdrop for extraordinary lighting and décor, such as a tent, community center or convention hall. Alternately, she says, "An ornately beautiful historic venue can provide you with all the décor you need, just by highlighting the existing architectural features."

Be Mysterious or Create the Marvelous

Hoyt says it is always helpful to make your event the first in a mysterious, private home or new facility, because guests will be curious to get inside. Seeking another alternative? "Transforming a venue that your guests are very familiar with (like a school gymnasium) into something unrecognizable and fantastic can have a huge impact as well," she says.

Tools, Tips and What You Should Avoid

Most convention and visitors bureaus have comprehensive event venue listings, as do local wedding planning sites, says Hoyt.

During the planning process, Hoyt says to: Pay attention to event industry news and event locations; look at open spaces with a discerning eye, knowing tents can be erected almost anywhere to create venue space; and keep an open mind.

One issue to be cautious about, Hoyt says, is available space as stated by the event venue. "Be wary of capacity charts when it comes to selecting a venue that is the appropriate size. Stages, buffets, silent auctions, dance floors and production equipment can take up a lot of space. Some salespeople overestimate maximum seating capacity to win the business, so be sure you consider the actual square footage as it relates to your event needs."

Seek Venues With Flexibility to Keep Costs Within Budget

Finally, Hoyt says, realize that nontraditional venues can be expensive when you add up extra costs (power, lighting, security, tenting). "Hotels can also be inflexible when it comes to cost-cutting, and it is important to include the added service charges in your budget," she says. "The most cost-effective venues are those with the flexibility to utilize vendors that you have relationships with and that are interested in supporting the mission of the nonprofit. Smaller private or nonprofit venues tend to have more flexibility than venues that have to answer to a higher corporate power."

Hoyt credits her success in venue choice largely to knowing people managing the venue would be helpful and responsive. "I try to consider venues with members of professional associations first," such as Meeting Professionals International, International Special Events Society and the National Association of Catering Executives, she says. "In most cases I have existing relationships with the people who work at the venue through membership involvement, and I already know that I like them and will enjoy working with them."

Source: Stacey Hoyt, Owner, Stacey Hoyt Events, Austin, TX.

Tip: *Woo your guests with an unusual or premier location. How about an artist's studio? Townhouses under construction? A members-only golf course?*

How to Plan Profitable, WOW-Factor Galas

BUDGETING & COST-CONSCIOUS ADVICE

Whether your gala is an annual affair or this is a first-time event, begin with a budget. Estimate both costs and anticipated revenue as your planning begins to unfold. A budget, even if based on estimates, helps you to see the big picture and determine what can be done to cut costs or increase revenue. There are also a number of steps you can take to keep gala expenses in line.

Budget Estimate Helps in Planning Stages

Before jumping into any new event, take the time to formulate a budget estimate complete with projected costs and revenue.

You need not be exact in projecting an event's expenses and revenue, but the very process of thinking through each component of your event will give you some idea of what may need to be done to project net income, increase revenue or decrease expenses. You may even decide that a particular event can't be justified based on the estimated budget.

The budget planning process will force you to make decisions about issues such as: program, entertainment, food/refreshments, venue, sources of revenue and more. That procedure will help you arrive at decisions that you may not fully consider in the absence of an event budget estimate.

Use the form shown below as a template to create your own event budget estimate. Share it with others on your staff or those helping with your event to get their input on anticipated costs and revenue.

Watching the Pennies: Creating an Event Budget

When creating a budget for your next event, follow this checklist for properly accounting for and tracking expenses:

- ❑ Work closely with your caterer to determine food and beverage costs. Don't forget to build in the cost of gratuity for the wait staff, which can be up to 20 percent above and beyond the caterer's total.

- ❑ If your event will require equipment rental, note all fees and build a cushion for cost of breakage and late fees.

- ❑ Itemize cost of gifts for guests, staff and/or volunteers. No matter how economical the gift, costs can add up due to number of items purchased.

- ❑ Calculate cost of transportation to include shuttles that may be provided to guests, as well as driver tips.

- ❑ When choosing the event site, obtain a bid from at least three potential sites to determine the best value. Build in extra for costs associated with early set up and tear down of the event.

- ❑ If you're holding your event outdoors, account for tent, table, chair and toileting facility rental.

- ❑ Allow for a contingency fund. Estimate approximately 10 to 20 percent of your total to a slush fund that allows for extras that were overlooked.

- ❑ Summarize your costs and review them again. Look meticulously for areas in which you can pare back to save expense without compromising on guest comfort or the quality of your event.

Content not available in this edition

Gala Spotlight ...

Set Goals to Make Your Annual Event an Ongoing Success

When you're talking maximum production at minimum price, the Cardinals have it. That is, The American Cardinals Dinner to fund scholarships at the Catholic University of America (Washington, D.C.).

The event has raised more than $26 million since its inception in 1989, with a goal of netting $1.2 million per year, says Frank Persico, vice president for university relations and chief of staff.

Persico says that the second goal organizers have for the event — keeping costs down to 22 cents on the dollar — helps achieve the first goal. That, and keeping in mind that the event "is a fundraiser not a spendraiser," he adds.

Persico shares some ways dinner organizers minimize costs to maximize proceeds:

- **Consider guests when planning events, and know that less can be more.** Persico says that, on occasion, they will have an after-dinner event, but only if it is warranted. When many guests are traveling to the dinner from long distances, for example, organizers will seek to arrange an after-dinner event. If not, that is an expense that is cut.

- **Recruit beneficiaries as volunteers.** Persico says 16 to 20 university seniors audition to volunteer for the event. "They act as human arrows, directing people to the places they need to go." They also donate three hours per week pre-event, help with transporting guests, escort the Cardinals to the dinner and speak about their university experiences. On occasion, students provide entertainment, which Persico says not only minimizes costs, it increases donations. Guests are able to hear firsthand how their donations are directly helping students at the university.

- **Set expectations up front.** Persico lets the Cardinals, student volunteers and other volunteers know up front what to expect. Cardinals pay their own transportation to get to the event. Volunteers' transportation expenses are covered, but they travel coach class and are provided with very basic hotel rooms.

Persico says that occasionally, people make a significant donation in lieu of attending the event, especially if they determine attending would cost them more, based on where the dinner is. He adds that even when attendance is low, they still raise significant funds by keeping costs down.

Source: Frank Persico, Vice President for University Relations and Chief of Staff, Catholic University of America, Washington, D.C. E-mail: persico@cua.edu

---

Stand-out Features Raise Profile of Event, University

The American Cardinals Dinner — started primarily as a fundraiser for the Catholic University of America (Washington, D.C.) — is also meant to raise the school's profile as the national university of the Catholic Church, says Vice President for University Relations and Chief of Staff Frank Persico.

To build awareness, Persico says, dinner organizers make the event as high-profile as possible while spotlighting all the university has to offer.

Ways they do so include:

✓ Holding the event at locations around the country to reach a broad range of people in various dioceses.

✓ Starting the event with a Mass celebrated by the hosting Archbishop and co-celebrated by the attending Cardinals. This is sometimes contrary to Catholic liturgical norms, making it a rare occasion, which raises the profile of the event.

✓ Including a receiving line where guests can meet and greet the Cardinal Archbishops, Cardinals Emeriti and Bishops.

✓ Giving guests easy access to the honorees by using a seating chart that places the church officials on the main floor with general guests.

✓ Crafting keepsake medallions for guests that feature the crest of the hosting Bishop or Archbishop on the front, the crest of the university on back and engraved signatures of each of the Cardinals.

Create First-time Event Budget

With so many factors to consider — from food to entertainment to decorations — how do you build a budget for a first-time event?

"The key is understanding costs for individual segments of the budget," says Cathy Genetti, president and founder of Next Level Event Design (Chicago, IL). "You need to know what to expect and what to budget for." Also, she says, have a not-to-exceed budget number as early in the planning process as possible.

Genetti shares steps she takes to help a nonprofit client determine a budget for a first-time fundraiser:

1. **Get a clear understanding of the organization's demographic**, events it has offered, the outcome of those events, and if they met expectations.

2. **Know the event goal**. The primary goal shouldn't be to raise money, but could be to create a closer community or increase awareness. Is there a call to action for the guests? What should be the emotional take-away?

3. **Articulate expectations and a shared definition of success.** Be realistic when planning an inaugural event and creating a count goal.

4. **Research other events in your area** that may impact attendance.

5. **Determine how much money the event is expected to raise**, then do the math. Are sponsors or sponsorship opportunities involved? What is an appropriate ticket price for this demographic? Will ticket price merely cover the cost of the per-person price? How will additional sums be raised?

6. **Estimate the hours needed to produce the event**, including meetings, conference calls, walk-throughs and production time. Overestimate to accommodate unknown issues.

7. **Check with stakeholders** to make sure the initial rough figure will work for them.

"Normally, there's one aspect of an event that is a main focus — it could be entertainment, food, lighting and décor, etc.," Genetti says. "Once you know this, you can earmark how much money you can allot to each category, so that you can give this information to your vendors."

Source: Cathy Genetti, President and Founder, Next Level Event Design, Chicago, IL.

Tips for Choosing a Caterer

If your special event requires a caterer, consider the following when selecting the caterer who is perfect for your event:

- **Check local directories to find caterers or ask for referrals** from other nonprofits that have offered premium events with the help of caterers.
- **Select at least three caterers to interview** with pricing options and food selections from which to choose.
- **Ask each catering service for references from within the past year.** Call on each reference and ask about quality, pricing and professionalism of each caterer.
- **Ask to review the caterer's portfolio** that shows food presentation and pictures of finished catered events.
- **Schedule a tasting.** Ask that each caterer offer a broad sampling of what he/she can offer your event.
- **Discuss your budget and weigh pricing carefully.** By no means is the price a caterer quotes you initially the final price. Work together to find cost-cutting measures to maintain quality but reduce costs.
- **Get it in writing.** Once pricing and service options are selected, ask for a final contract with the caterer and review it well in advance of the event. Don't hesitate to ask questions and review the fine print to ensure you're not left with hidden costs.

Tip: When seeking speakers for your event, begin in your immediate area. Finding a local expert to speak at an event will save your organization in travel fees, per diems and hotel stays.

Tips Help Save Money Throughout All Aspects of Your Event

Mazarine Treyz (Austin, TX) is a nonprofit management consultant and author of the book and blog, "The Wild Woman's Guide to Fundraising."

Here, she shares tips on how to save money on your fundraising event.

- ❏ **Get the word out through free services, such as local radio.** Get an interview about your event on your local community radio station. To find one, enter your city name and the term community radio into your favorite online search engine. You can also try going to your local television station to get a free interview for your event. If you cannot get an interview, get your event listed.

- ❏ **Invest in effective advertising and communications resource materials.** In need of free publicity and/or sponsorship? Save on the costs of buying a mailing list by purchasing just one special book. Your regional "Business Journal's Book of Lists" can be a good resource for finding new companies to approach for supporting your cause. (Using your favorite online search engine, enter your state's name, and the phrase, Business Journal Book of Lists.) The publication features lists of top companies arranged by industry and a listing of key decision makers and their contact information. Treyz offers a free presentation about how to obtain sponsorships at www.wildwomanfundraising.com/how-do-you-get-an-event-sponsorship. After you have your sponsorship, get your mailing list and go for co-branding opportunities on your website and on their website.

- ❏ **Leverage your loyalty.** Go to the same printer every time and negotiate a lower price based on your loyalty and the urgency of your cause. Try negotiating a lower price for T-shirts, pens, buttons, etc. to give out or sell at your event.

- ❏ **Look for fresh, hungry talent to help promote your event.** To receive discounted design work, find a graphic design student interested in doing graphic design for you at a reasonable price. (Be careful about hiring a designer as an intern without pay. Certain legalities surround the issue of not paying interns, even for nonprofit organizations. For more information, read "The Legalities of Nonprofit Internships" by Ellen Aldridge at www.blueavocado.org/content/legalities-nonprofit-internships).

- ❏ **Engage free help with event-related tasks.** Get volunteers to stuff invitation envelopes for you. In Canada, post an opportunity at www.volunteer.ca. Try Workforce Solutions in Austin, TX, and Steps to Success in Portland, OR. Otherwise, try www.volunteermatch.com. Need a stage manager? Need an usher? Post volunteer opportunities everywhere you can (e.g., local high schools, colleges and universities and websites like www.beextra.org).

- ❏ **Tap multiple sources for donations of items and services needed for your special event.** For donations of food and venue space, use your board member connections. Consider anyone who has given to your event before. Another resource can be a new restaurant in town, or a new catering service. For example, ask them if they'd like to have a table at your event with their cards and displays in exchange for free hors d'oeuvres. Show them you can help them reach their audience, and they'll be more interested in at least donating an in-kind product.

- ❏ **Learn from the experts in your community.** Don't hesitate to seek out the free advice available from the individuals at SCORE, the Service Corps of Retired Executives (www.score.org). They can offer suggestions on everything from event logistics to budget management. You can take a class or get free counseling.

Source: Mazarine Treyz, Wild Woman Fundraising, Austin, TX.
E-mail: info@wildwomanfundraising.com

Tip: After booking the location for your gala, find out who will be using that space ahead of you. They may have certain materials — decorations, lighting, equipment and more — that would work in nicely with your event.

Tip: *Don't sign a speaker's contract without negotiating first. Because of the economy, many speakers are quite willing to consider alternative offers: decreased speaking fees, travel expenses, additional services and more.*

Low-cost Ways to Spruce Up Your Event

One sure-fire way to increase event revenue is to cut costs up front.

James Reber (San Jose, CA), a professional fundraising consultant and special event producer with 30-plus years of experience in the nonprofit sector, suggests cutting costs of food and beverages — typically an event's biggest expenses — by asking for donations or reduced rates. On that note, he adds, search for a public relations professional willing to donate his or her time to help with marketing, which can be another major expense.

Samantha Swaim, director/event strategist, Samantha Swaim Fundraising LLC (Portland, OR), says to invest in lighting to lower your decorating budget. "A little up-lighting in your room can be a quick way to transform a space. Instead of big entry drapes and arches, think simple and use lighting to create ambience. It's cheaper and more effective."

A theme, Swain says, is another low-cost way to spur enthusiasm. "A fun theme can get the ideas flowing and add the creative spark you need to dress things up a bit."

Ticket costs are another consideration. Are your revenues down because you're not charging enough to attend?

Judy Sitzer, owner of New Philanthropy Group (Santa Monica, CA), says organizations should compare their ticket costs to those of other events in the area, weighing exactly how much people receive for the price of admission.

Sources: James Reber, Professional Fundraising Consultant and Special Event Producer, San Jose, CA. E-mail: james@jamesreber.com
Judy Sitzer, Owner, New Philanthropy Group, Santa Monica, CA.
E-mail: judy@newphilanthropygroup.com
Samantha Swaim, Director/Event Strategist, Samantha Swaim Fundraising LLC, Portland, OR.
E-mail: sam@samanthaswaim.com

Scale Back Your Gala Without Sacrificing Style

Finding subtle ways to tastefully scale back a special event will make your guests feel more comfortable during hard times, and may even increase your ticket sales.

Kathleen Norton-Schock, vice president of marketing, Michigan Council of Women in Technology (Auburn Hills, MI), hosts an annual gala that is the group's signature event and one of its top fundraisers. "Our events still attract donors," Norton-Schock says, "and sponsorship has not been as difficult for us as it has been for others during the recession."

To scale back a major event yet still keep donors, Norton-Schock recommends switching from formal to semi-formal attire, which tells guests they won't need to spend money on tuxedos or new dresses, yet still indicates the event will have a high-end flair.

Offer arriving guests a drink, she says, but scale down costs by limiting kinds of alcohol being served. Instead of an open bar, give a choice of red or white wine, creating a more relaxed, intimate environment while giving people common ground to initiate a conversation (e.g., "I see you chose the white wine, too! This is one of my favorites.").

Fill as many event jobs as possible with volunteers. Norton-Schock says council galas are always "100 percent volunteer-run." A hired staff of jacketed bartenders telegraphs stuffiness, while having friends and associates pouring drinks eliminates stuffiness, saves money and provides the opportunity for communication between donors and volunteers.

Lastly, to boost people's interest and increase attendance, Norton-Schock recommends having a big-name guest of honor in attendance — and featuring his/her name prominently on the invitation. People who work in Michigan's technology sector often attend the MCWT's events; when a locally based guest of honor such as a GM or Ford executive is noted on the invitation, the gala becomes a priceless networking opportunity.

Source: Kathleen Norton-Schock, Vice President-Marketing, Michigan Council of Women in Technology, Auburn Hills, MI. E-mail: knorton-schock@ardentcause.com

How to Plan Profitable, WOW-Factor Galas

Communicate With Florist to Maximize Value, Match Mood

While flowers may be seasonal, the impact they add to special events is timeless.

Flowers can also be one of the major overhead expenses. To maximize your investment in ambience and retain dollars that can benefit your programs:

- ✓ **Choose a florist appropriate to event size.** Your corner flower shop may be perfect for creating a floral spray for the head table at your employee tea, but you need more flower power for your annual gala's 50 centerpieces. Larger events require more staff, refrigeration, reliable delivery and setup of a sometimes-fragile product.
- ✓ **Plan floral arrangements well in advance.** A preflight consultation with your floral expert and flexibility in the final product can bring big savings. Decide which blossoms will be the best value at the time of your event, then talk spray treatments, trimming and container colors to match your theme. A red palette with sprayed carnations may accomplish the same goal as more costly roses.
- ✓ **Negotiate little extras.** Ask the florist about an all-inclusive package where you agree to a set price for each centerpiece, topiary or swag, but get corsages or boutonnieres for honorees in the bargain. See if florists could waive rental or setup fees for non-floral items like trellises, urns and stands in exchange for posting a sign at the event that says "Display Items courtesy of Downtown Florists."
- ✓ **Ask about repeat business discounts.** Review the past few years of flower purchases. Include those repeated annually in a contract bid for floral services for six months to a year. While you will pay extra for needs outside the contract, many shops will be eager to give you the best possible deal on other floral services, such as thank-you baskets for special supporters, when they know you are coming back.
- ✓ **Evaluate when a nursery can do double duty.** Can potted geraniums and dahlias destined for your facility's planters first be used as centerpieces for your spring luncheon? An accommodating nursery can wrap the pots in festive foil for your party before they are turned over to the groundskeeper.

Tip: *To make your event affordable to people of different income levels, sell three levels of tickets that each have their own perks — valet parking, special seating and more.*

Save on Event Expenses With Up-and-coming Photographers

If you are looking for a photographer to shoot your next event or capture some great shots for your annual report, consider using a student or someone new to the field, suggests Nicole Knight, director of marketing and communications, Army and Navy Academy (Carlsbad, CA).

"We connect with or try to hire photographers or college students who are new to the industry or their careers to photograph our events for a much smaller stipend," says Knight. The result? "Quality shots for half the price."

She says she finds photographers through word of mouth, Craigslist and university intern programs. Costs range from photographers willing to work solely for the experience or in exchange for credits for their internship and a letter of recommendation, to ones who charge up to $50 per hour.

Knight works with two to three photographers per year, ensuring she doesn't wear out any one photographer, affording her backup in case someone is sick and giving a wider range of perspective. "Different photographers have different ideas and shoot from a variety of angles — or perhaps like to play with different lighting or focal points," she says.

Knight acknowledges that some risk is involved in going with an unknown, but notes that preparation can offset that.

Don't simply send the photographer to your event to take pictures, she says. Go over specific expectations to help ensure the results are what you expect and need.

"Factor in 15 to 20 minutes to discuss the best locations for your photographer to stand, who the key people are that you would like them to catch and the most important part of the events," Knight says, "so they're not off snapping shots of decorations during the president's speech."

Source: Nicole Knight, Director of Marketing and Communications, Army and Navy Academy, Carlsbad, CA. E-mail: nknight@armyandnavyacademy.org

Know When to Turn to Professional Event Security

With nonprofits underfunded and event planners understaffed, event security is often one of the first expenses to be cut. That's a big mistake, says Karl Bradey, founder of Total Protection Services, Inc. (Indianapolis, IN). "People don't think about security until something happens, but then it's too late," he says. "Providing a safe environment should be the first thing you do."

If you're considering professional security for an upcoming event, the expected number of attendees is one of the first factors you should take into account. Contrary to what many think, event security is as much about crowd management as crime prevention, says Bradey. "Keeping people moving in the right direction and not congregating at inopportune places is a large part of what we do," he says.

The profile of featured attendees is another key factor. "Any time you have a high-status celebrity who draws a big following, you're going to need security," says Bradey, adding that while most celebrities bring their own security, they will also want local staff who are more familiar with the venue.

Event planners sometimes use volunteers in security roles as a way to cut costs. This can be appropriate in some circumstances, but unwise in others, says Bradey. "Volunteers are fine for guarding access points for entry purposes, but crowd management should always be left to paid professionals."

Using armed versus unarmed guards is another important decision, and one on which Bradey has clear advice: "Pretty much the only time I recommend armed security is when money needs to be protected," he says. He notes that introducing weapons into a crowded venue can often make conditions less safe, not more. "Ninety percent of my work is unarmed, and competent security personnel can handle most situations without a weapon."

> ### Police Vs. Security: Whom to Use When
>
> Police and private security services work hand-in-hand, but it is helpful to know the role of each, says Karl Bradey, founder of Total Protection Services, Inc. (Indianapolis, IN) and a police officer himself.
>
> "The biggest difference is that police officers are more legally restricted than security officers," says Bradey. "Police will not work in any venue that is serving liquor. They also mostly only touch people when they are making an arrest, so they prefer not to get involved with crowd management. Security personnel are often more effective for working in close quarters."
>
> Bradey says police officers can be effective in protecting parking lots, enforcing the law when necessary, and maintaining a level of visibility to discourage trouble before it starts.
>
> According to Brady, many large venues require a minimum number of police officers at events of certain types and sizes, thereby taking the decision out of event planners' hands. He also says security officers will cost only about half what police officers do.

When selecting a security company, Bradey says to consider references, history, background and type of events serviced, but to also make sure the organization has a standardized training program in areas like personal protection, self-defense and communication skills.

He also advises sticking with a company once you have established a satisfactory relationship. "When officers come back year after year, they will know what your organization is, how your event operates and what your crowd demographics are. That's beneficial for both you and them."

Source: Karl Bradey, Founder, Total Protection Services, Inc., Indianapolis, IN.
E-mail: Kbradey65@gmail.com

Gala Spotlight ...

Chauffeured Scavenger Hunt Draws Business Participation

In its fifth year, the House of Refuge (Mesa, AZ) Chauffeured Scavenger Hunt Gala draws an average attendance of 250 participants.

The House of Refuge works to support homeless individuals by offering transitional housing, supportive resources and a program teaching self-sufficiency and sustainability. The annual limo scavenger event supports these efforts by raising nearly $41,000 through ticket sales ($100 each), a silent auction and private limousine sponsorships ($1,500 each).

The primary focus of the evening is the competitive chauffeured scavenger hunt, where teams pile into one of the 25 sponsored limousines and seek out items on the scavenger list. The event takes approximately two-and-a-half hours and includes tasks such as answering trivia questions, following clues to find items throughout the city and/or taking a photo of list items. One example is finding a fire station that will allow participants to hop on the fire truck and get a snapshot (a firehouse with a dog yields extra points.) Each item or question scores points, which are tabulated at the end of the hunt to award prizes.

"This event is a great team-building exercise for local business owners and managers," says Kristine Devine, event chair. "We have many groups return each year from law offices, mortgage companies and other professional businesses to use this as a team building exercise."

Devine offers her most useful tips for organizing a chauffeured scavenger hunt event:

At a Glance —	
Event Type:	Limousine Scavenger Hunt
Gross:	$41,000
Costs:	$13,000
Net Income:	$28,000
Volunteers:	20
Planning:	12 months
Attendees:	250
Revenue Sources:	Ticket sales, limousine sponsorships, silent auction and event program advertising
Unique Feature:	Competitive chauffeured scavenger hunt

- **Don't attempt to haggle with the limo company.** The limousine contract is not where you want to trim costs, says Devine. The limos are the pinnacle of the event and because a large number of them are necessary to pull off the event with style, the booking limo service will need to outsource limos from other providers. Therefore, you do not want to undercut the provider which could undermine the level of service provided at the event.

- **Check your contract carefully for the limo driver tipping standard.** Many limousine contracts will include tipping for the driver within the price of your package, so extra tipping is not required. Recommend to guests that they're welcome to tip their driver if they've received extraordinary service, but also let them know that tipping is included within the contract agreement.

- **Create limo sponsorships that align with advertising in the event program.** At this scavenger hunt, the planning committee offers a half-page ad with each limousine sponsorship to support the sponsorship function of the event.

Source: Kristine Devine, Event Chair, House of Refuge, Mesa, AZ.
E-mail: Kristine@devineproperties.com

Uncorking the Profit on Wine-tasting Events

What can a nonprofit do to generate even more revenue from its wine tasting event?

One nonprofit sharing advice is The Riverbanks Society (Columbia, SC). On April 23, 2010, this nonprofit organization, which supports the needs of Riverbanks Zoo and Garden (Columbia, SC), hosted its seventh annual Wine Tasting event.

To gain better success this year compared to previous years, Events Manager Lochlan Kennedy says that costs were better controlled.

"Gaining inventory control — knowing what quantity/ varieties distributors are bringing well in advance is key," Kennedy says. "When you're getting wine donated, you can often have little control over how much you are receiving and when."

Another factor contributing to the event's success was the venue choice — the scenic Riverbanks Botanical Garden (Columbia, SC).

In addition, rather than hiring an outside firm to pour the wine, "We had volunteer pourers, so that the vintners/distributors could talk about wine," Kennedy says.

But, Kennedy says, especially key in gaining increasing profitability was the acquisition of sponsorships. Kennedy says that sponsorships often result from networks that have already been built. For those starting from scratch, or without those networks, she says the key is doing the research to find the right strategic partners. "Our strategy was to pinpoint the corporations and entities that might be interested." Kennedy says. This ranged from large corporations such as Time Warner, to banks and retail stores.

Source: Lochlan Kennedy, Events Manager, Riverbanks Zoo and Garden, Columbia, SC.
E-mail: lkennedy@riverbanks.org

How to Plan Profitable, WOW-Factor Galas

VOLUNTEER & BOARD INVOLVEMENT

Since board and volunteer involvement is key to any gala's success, the ways in which you select, engage, organize and nurture volunteers at every level are vitally important. The number of volunteers you involve will impact attendance. Your selection of volunteers and the assignments you give them will impact the quality of the event. Have a comprehensive list of volunteer opportunities along with an organizational structure early in the game.

Tip: To make planning your event more fun for everyone involved, incorporate portions of the event into the planning process.

Tip: If a member of your gala's planning team criticizes you, ask how he/she would handle a similar situation. This disengages a potential confrontation and leads toward a solution.

Bring Experienced Leaders to the Table, Solicit Their Expertise

Attracting busy and sought-after community leaders to volunteer for your next important event is a tall order that requires understanding the background and interests of those individuals and taking time to learn about their philanthropic priorities. Here are some ways to start making contact and building relationships.

Identify five people with whom you hope to work with. Remember that while these individuals might be admired, popular and capable, they may already be involved with other organizations. But if it's clear that their skills and passions have a place in your programs or services, write them a letter citing specific examples of how your organization needs them — and why their time will be well-spent with you.

Host a volunteer summit to identify community needs. Ask your own board members and volunteer leaders to spearhead the event, but leave the format open for input from other leaders. Invite 50 or 100 representatives from business, government and other nonprofits to hear your long-range goals and make recommendations. Once they have become familiar with your organization, an invitation to become more involved is a natural transition.

Offer complimentary event tickets to get acquainted. Begin planning your next gala by inviting possible future chairmen. They may have attended with friends before, but make sure these complimentary seats come directly from your office. This will give you an opportunity to introduce yourself before the event, to make contact at the party and to make a follow-up call asking if they enjoyed themselves or have suggestions for improvement. Their feedback will help you determine where their expertise can be best utilized.

Your Chairperson Can Make (or Break) an Event

Think of finding the best chairperson for your next event like being on a treasure hunt. Is there a diamond in the rough in your pool of likely volunteers who has the experience and dedication to help reach the highest level of success?

Review this checklist to decide who best fits the profile of a results-oriented leader:

- ❑ Has this individual been an active supporter long enough to understand your mission and be familiar with your volunteer resources?
- ❑ Will his/her other volunteer activities conflict with the role you have in mind?
- ❑ Can this person meet deadlines and motivate others to complete tasks on time?
- ❑ Is the candidate known and respected by others who might be asked to volunteer?
- ❑ Does this individual possess what it takes to enlist and motivate others?
- ❑ Will the individual's other priorities — work, family, travel requirements — blend well with the job's requirements?
- ❑ Is the person better described as a skillful delegator or a micromanager who insists on being involved in every decision?
- ❑ Will the person need a lot of direction or hand-holding that could keep you from completing more crucial responsibilities?
- ❑ Does he/she possess skills needed to keep conflicts from turning into tense situations?
- ❑ Does the person possess the confidence to make tough decisions and stay focused on outcomes?

Recruit and Manage Volunteers for Your Next Special Event

Recruiting special event volunteers allows your organization to plan events in an organized fashion with strong oversight. Officials with March of Dimes (Kalamazoo, MI) recruit special event volunteers to manage every detail of their events.

"The role of a special event volunteer is to serve the organization in a variety of capacities," says Dana DeLuca, March of Dimes division director. "Whether it be handling pre-event administrative tasks, serving as a committee member, cultivating event revenue or overseeing the event logistics, the special event volunteer is multi-faceted and plays an essential role in the overall success of an event. The most challenging task is finding the right role for each volunteer, managing to their strengths and giving them the tools to succeed and to feel successful."

DeLuca offers tips to recruit and manage volunteers for your special event:

❑ **Make the ask.** People can only respond if asked, and volunteer-minded persons are likely to offer something to your nonprofit. More often than not, says DeLuca, the volunteer with the most staying power has been asked to join the organization in a volunteer capacity to help move the mission forward.

❑ **Determine the volunteer's specialty.** Find what motivates each individual volunteer and assign him/her to opportunities according to those strengths. "It pays to find out what people are looking to gain from their role as volunteers and to help match them up with opportunities that best complement their desire to give back," says DeLuca.

❑ **Give them the tools to succeed and get out of their way.** Through the March of Dimes Volunteer Leadership Institute, an executive leadership program helps volunteers become experts in the organization. The program helps in recruiting and retaining strong board members, having successful events and providing effective programming. Tools offered to volunteers include educational items such as the publications shown below that illustrate where gifts go and provide basic information about the March of Dimes so volunteers can speak in an informed way at special events.

Providing volunteers with educational items such as these helps prepare them to speak at special events on behalf of the March of Dimes (Portage, MI).

Source: Dana DeLuca, Division Director, March of Dimes, Portage, MI.
E-mail: ddeluca@marchofdimes.com

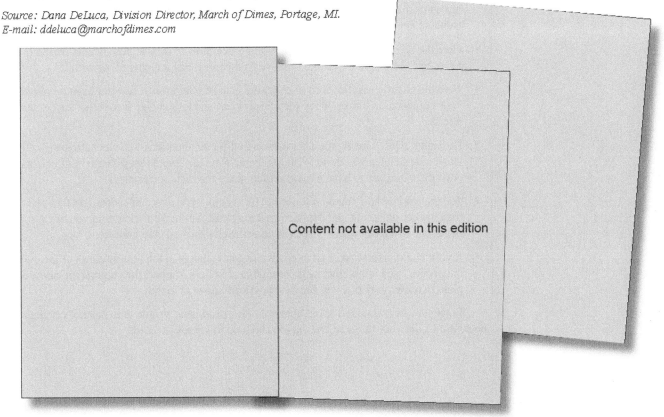

Content not available in this edition

Event Within Event Boosts Honorary Committee

To boost the value of membership on your honorary committee, host an event within an event exclusively for its members.

Executive Director Maureen O'Brien-Thornton says The Leukemia & Lymphoma Society, Upstate New York/Vermont Chapter (Albany, NY) has done this by including a Sommelier Throwdown as part of its Taste of Compassion wine-tasting event.

This VIP event, moderated by a locally renowned food columnist, is a private wine tasting with three area sommeliers, each of whom brings a selection of wine. Honorary committee ticket holders sample and vote on the specially selected wines.

Honorary committee members pay $125 each to become a part of the committee and, says O'Brien-Thornton, the throwdown has become a coveted benefit of their position.

She adds that this special addition has boosted both fundraising from honorary committee donations and increased repeat service by honorary committee members.

Source: Maureen O'Brien-Thornton, Executive Director, the Leukemia & Lymphoma Society, Upstate New York/Vermont Chapter, Albany, NY. E-mail: Maureen.Thornton@lls.org

Prepare Event Chairperson to Boost Confidence, Success

Once you identify and enlist the best volunteer as an event or committee chairperson, it's equally important that you provide him/her with the level of training and support needed to carry out responsibilities with confidence and ease.

Follow these suggestions to become the best possible person to make your chairperson's job run smoothly:

- Don't assume the chairperson knows every member of your staff or every member of your volunteer committee or every aspect of your cause. Educate the person to get him/her up to speed and capable of taking charge of this important event that will draw both valuable community support and needed funds for your cause.

- Give the chairperson solid guidelines and procedures to follow, but also the freedom necessary to be innovative and creative so the event has impetus for growth.

- Give the chairperson freedom to enlist the help of others who have not been involved in your organization before. They may bring ideas and knowledge from other successful events.

- Be candid when alerting the chairperson to difficult situations you can anticipate, or about past failures you don't wish to repeat. Warn him/her about potential pitfalls, and encourage him/her to have a backup plan ready for such occurrences.

- Tell the chairperson you do not need to be consulted on every decision, and that you trust his/her judgment and decision-making skills, but make it clear that you always have time to answer questions, even ones the chairperson may consider trivial.

- If your chairperson makes an executive decision that is in the best interests of the event but proves to be unpopular with committee members, support the chairperson and explain to others why this was the best possible course of action.

Finally, be open-minded about approaching a promising person who has not yet chaired an event. Under your tutelage, the person can help the event succeed.

Tip: For your special event committee, keep leadership balanced by picking co-chairs with different connections.

Choose one cochair from internal sources — such as your board — for the experience he/she brings to the table. Choose the second from the community — for the influence factor. To establish an even wider base of support for your event and your cause, choose co-chairs who run in different circles and are different ages.

Gala Spotlight ...

Four Tips for Gala Success Will Make You Believe in Magic

When your guests tell others about your special event, you hope they will praise the amazing food, awesome speaker and stellar entertainment. But above all, you hope your guests will remember — and share — how the event made a difference in peoples' lives.

Organizers of the Wish Night annual gala for Make-A-Wish Foundation of North Texas (Irving, TX) make sure attendees remember what the event is all about by focusing all aspects on the organization's mission of fulfilling wishes for seriously ill children, says Erin Michel, development director-central region.

"We don't pay for outside entertainment," Michel says. "Our 'wish' kids share their experiences and do an original performance based on the event's theme. You leave knowing exactly what you were there for."

The event has netted more than $7 million since 1997, Michel says, noting factors that contribute to its success:

❑ **A strong and organized volunteer committee.** "This is the bread and butter of the event. We have about 30 people, including a ball chair, on several smaller committees," each with a cochair who rotates into the chair in subsequent years.

❑ **A dedicated staff person.** A staff person whose sole function is the annual gala gives volunteers consistent support.

❑ **Show-stopping auction items and a superb auctioneer.** "It's really important to think outside the box about what is going to be a stellar item for auctions," says Michel. Some of this year's items include more than $100,000 in diamonds thanks to the Zale Corporation, a sleepover in Nastia Liukin's gym and a VIP experience with the Dallas Mavericks.

❑ **Building up excitement.** At least two additional events lead up to the annual gala, including a kickoff party and auction preview party, along with a formal check presentation about one month after the event. These provide multiple opportunities to increase visibility, generate media excitement and involve constituents.

Source: Erin Michel, Development Director-Central Region, Make-A-Wish Foundation of North Texas, Irving, TX.
E-mail: emichel@northtexaswish.org

At a Glance —

Event Type:	Black-tie gala
Gross:	$1,259,152
Costs:	$233,929
Net Income:	$1,025,223
Volunteers:	200-plus
Planning:	12 months
Attendees:	1,100
Revenue Sources:	Ticket sales, sponsorships, live and silent auctions, raffle
Unique Feature:	Show-stopping auction items such as a VIP experience with a professional basketball team

Targeted Committees Make Event Successful

Numbers from the Make-A-Wish Foundation of North Texas (Irving, TX) Wish Night are mind boggling: Some 1,110 people attend the event organized primarily by 200 volunteers, with 100 sponsors and 800 auction items.

This recipe has raised more than $7 million in 12 years.

The key ingredient to the event's success? Volunteers.

Thirty volunteers serve on eight committees with 15 subcommittees, handling everything from décor to sponsor asks to catering and marketing, breaking the major event into manageable steps, says Erin Michel, development director-central region.

To structure event-planning committees, Michel says:

✓ **Be specific.** Have job descriptions that include responsibilities prior to, during and after the event. Include all the jobs that no one wants to do, but have to get done (e.g., cleaning auction items the night of the event, transporting items back to the office, etc.). Include details that are taken for granted, leaving no room for error (e.g., who does each person report to, what meetings are they required to attend, what records are they expected to keep).

✓ **Have a succession plan.** Why start from scratch every year? Make sure most folks signing on are interested in a multi-year commitment. Make sure every committee has cochairs to rotate in to the chair position over the next two years, giving you three year's of stability. This allows you to focus on growing the event, not just finding warm bodies.

✓ **Keep detailed records.** Require all committee chairs and cochairs to keep detailed records of their activities, functions and any tips.

Confirm Volunteer Assignments in Writing

As you work with multiple volunteers on events requiring their individual follow-up, improve the odds of their completing assigned tasks by providing each volunteer with written confirmation of what it is he/she is supposed to do and by when.

Whenever you conduct a meeting in which volunteers leave with agreed-to tasks, immediately send each volunteer a personalized memo — as opposed to a standardized group memo — confirming his or her specific duties. Spell out exactly what is expected of the volunteer, the persons to contact if the volunteer has any questions and the deadline for the project (or multiple deadlines for portions of the project).

In addition to listing each task to be completed, be clear on the ways in which to report back or turn in completed work. This helps bring closure to the task.

Here are two techniques you may want to include in your memo:

1. Offer an incentive for completing tasks on time.

2. Add a final sentence to your memo indicating that all persons not completing their tasks by the stated deadline will be contacted by you (or the appropriate person) to determine what needs to happen in order to finish the project. Adding a closing statement such as this motivates volunteers to avoid the embarrassment of being contacted, while, providing you with a justifiable reason for following up with them.

Use this example of a memo confirming a volunteer's duties to craft individualized messages to key volunteers for your special events.

Follow Up With Persons Unable to Attend a Meeting

While some may argue it's the responsibility of persons who miss meetings to find out what they missed, it's clearly in your best interest to see that such persons are updated promptly and thoroughly. To do so:

- Make it a point to meet with or call those unable to attend within two or three days after a missed meeting.

- Summarize key meeting points and go over information that requires their attention and follow up. Give deadlines.

Even though non-attendees should be expected to follow up on meetings on their own, know that your initiative to connect with them conveys the importance of what was missed and keeps alive their responsibilities to complete assigned tasks.

Jan. 3, 2012

St. Joseph's Hospital FOUNDATION

TO: Tom Peterson, Sponsorship Committee
FROM: Brenda M. Hawley, Sponsorship Chairperson
RE: Calls to Be Completed By Feb. 15
CC: Debra M. Brown, Director of Alumni

Thank you, Tom, for attending the Dec. 13 Sponsorship Committee meeting and agreeing to call on the following businesses to serve as sponsors for our upcoming event.

As you know, it's imperative that we have commitments from these businesses by Feb. 15 if we are to remain on schedule with our event timeline. For that reason, I am suggesting you schedule appointments for this week and next so business owners and managers have sufficient time to make a decision.

Please turn in (or fax) your completed calls to the Office of Alumni as you complete them. The fax number is 465-9097. As was mentioned at our meeting, those who turn in all calls on time will receive two 50 percent off coupons for dinner at Winchester's.

I encourage you to call me or Debra Brown if you have any questions, need any assistance or experience any difficulty that would impede your ability to complete these calls on schedule.

I will plan to contact any persons who have not turned in their calls to the Office of Alumni by Feb. 15.

Thank you for your valuable assistance with this portion of our 2010 Celebrity Speaker Event.

Sponsorship Calls to be Completed by Tom Peterson by Feb. 15:

- Benders Office Supply & Equipment
- Determan Pepsi Distributors
- Osborne Trucking, Inc.
- Klein Brokers
- Castrole Travel
- Peterson Photography
- MasterCuts
- Winston Raceway

Emcee Duos Bring Chemistry, Fun To Your Fundraiser

Two heads are better than one for brainstorming, and it also may be true when choosing a master of ceremonies for your next special event. Instead of asking one dynamic personality, ask two — making sure they will work well together and off each other to your event's advantage.

Here are some advantages to asking an emcee duo to keep the show moving and the audience entertained.

- ❑ **Increased audience participation.** One emcee is usually confined to a stage, but two can easily spread out and involve more people in the festivities with wireless microphones.
- ❑ **Flexibility with unexpected events.** When an inevitable technical glitch or delay occurs, your emcee team may be better prepared to fill the void by engaging guests in conversation, spontaneously getting them on stage or simply asking them why they support your cause.
- ❑ **Shared program preparations.** The best emcees come well-briefed on key guests, supporters and performers. While one is boning up on honoree backgrounds, the other can study your institution's culture and history.
- ❑ **Complementary skills and chemistry.** Dean Martin and Jerry Lewis were successful on their own, but had lightning in a bottle as a duo. The right emcee team can bring the same kind of enjoyment to your audiences, as long as the humor stays lighthearted and PG-rated.
- ❑ **Reading and responding to audience reactions.** It's easier to observe guests' moods with a team. Are they getting restless or sneaking out while pretending to get a drink? Picking up the program pace is more seamless when boredom can be humorously acknowledged by two emcees.
- ❑ **Easier use of props and costumes.** Since both emcees don't need to be on stage at the same time, there are more opportunities for using props, changing clothes or making transitions from one part of a program to another.

Have Event Backup Plan in Case Chair Drops Out

The success of any important charitable event depends upon an effective chairperson and a team of experienced volunteers — not the chairperson alone. If for any reason the chairperson of your event suddenly departs, a backup plan including the following strategies will keep the effort moving with minimal disruption:

- ✓ **Prepare your vice chair.** This person will attend all major planning sessions and receive the same information and contact names as the general chair, ideally with the plan that he or she will serve as chair the following year.
- ✓ **Ask past chairs to be advisors.** If they are willing, a team of past chairs can rally to assist the person who must assume the ex-chairperson's duties.
- ✓ **Gather committee co-chairs.** Determine which committees are best prepared to take over various tasks, dividing the duties as equally as possible.
- ✓ **Be alert for signs of difficulty.** There may be advance warnings that your chair is unable or unwilling to complete all steps necessary to ensure a successful event. Absences from meetings, lack of enthusiasm or negativity toward others' ideas can be signals that a new game plan is in order.
- ✓ **Remain diplomatic and nonjudgmental if your chair withdraws for non-emergency reasons.** Attempting to discuss the situation with outside parties will only derail you from the more important mission of getting plans back on track quickly.
- ✓ **Promote your new chair.** You may be able to parlay the change in personnel into an opportunity for extra publicity. Write press releases announcing the new chairperson, emphasizing his/her volunteer experience, dedication and enthusiasm for your event. The publicity may even attract new volunteers who thought it was too late for them to help.

Tip: To beef up the attractiveness of serving on an event's cleanup committee, offer a special incentive for persons who sign up for this task. For example, take away an obligation to attend other meetings or offer cleanup team members a free centerpiece or post-cleanup meal.

Make the Most of a Volunteer Publicity Committee

As you evaluate the publicity needs for your special event, evaluate your volunteer corps as well. Do you have volunteers whose background or talents are a good match for a specific type of publicity?

Even in large organizations, it's most effective to think small when recruiting volunteers to serve on your publicity committee. One well-rounded and experienced individual, accompanied by an assistant chairman, may be more than adequate for some events.

If your major event or slate of several upcoming events will require more extensive publicity efforts, think first of the categories of coverage you hope to attract:

- **Television, radio and newspapers.** Public service announcements, press releases and photographs are among the most useful vehicles for informing the community of your events. A person who writes news releases well and who can draft copy for radio announcements will be a valuable addition to your committee. Even if the volunteer has never had professional experience in these areas, possessing the skill to write concise facts for editors and producers to use will be appreciated.

- **Your organization's ambassador.** Every organization has an individual who has friends and contacts to enlist to help your cause. This person may have excellent telephone skills and be diligent about follow-up calls to media or sponsors who have agreed to help you with publicity. A community liaison with broad-based knowledge of publicity resources should be the primary contact for media, which helps avoid the number of duplicate calls received by others on your committee.

- **Attractive presentation of publicity proposals.** Once you have found individuals who can communicate well both on paper and in person, a designer, decorator or artistic person can round out the group. The combination of well-written facts, attractive graphics for printed materials or promotional posters, and a pleasant individual to present them to media representatives will help your organization stand above those who simply call or mail news releases.

Tip: Whether it's the CEO, board chairperson or someone else, your event's host should be at the front entrance greeting people as they arrive. Depending on the event's type, valet parking can also add to a positive first impression.

Coordinating Internal and External Publicity

Go beyond matching volunteers to publicity tasks, as detailed above, to make sure your employees know details of special events as well.

When paid staff produce newsletters and brochures for activities, involve them in the volunteer efforts to increase the impact of your combined efforts.

Paid staff and volunteers both bring expertise to the table, and a volunteer may have a more flexible schedule to meet with media at the media's convenience. By the same token, one of your paid staff may have professional media contacts who would be willing to work with your organization's volunteer.

Look at all resources within your organization, whether they are offered by volunteers or staff. Pair them when the combination of skills and chemistry is logical to save time and increase creative energy.

Have a clear description of duties for each member of the publicity committee so each member knows what he/she should pursue, and what his/her fellow committee members are doing. Should they decide between themselves that one is better suited than another for a specific duty, allow them the flexibility they need to achieve the publicity objective as long as everyone is agreeable.

Structure and clear job descriptions are important guides for volunteers, but good chemistry and common interest in obtaining the best possible coverage for your event are the best qualifications for volunteers on the publicity committee.

Your involvement is important to them as a resource and a guide, but if you have asked the best-qualified persons to serve, all you will really need are regular updates on their progress, and to be sure they have support they need from other volunteers and staff.

Gala Spotlight ...

Setting is Picture-perfect for Area's Highly Social Summer Scene

Each summer, Saratoga, NY, crackles with the excitement of thoroughbred horse racing. When the sun sets, the party continues with charity events and benefits galore. To stand out from the pack, nonprofits must pull out all the stops.

Nicole DeCelle, associate director, signature events, Albany Medical Center Foundation (Albany, NY) says they have done so with their annual Light Up the Night event.

The premiere summer event takes place at Saratoga National Golf Club. Guests are greeted with a champagne station as they make their way upstairs to the grand ballroom, where guests can mingle and enjoy uniquely themed food stations, passed hors d'oeuvres and specialty drinks provided by award-winning executive chefs.

As sunset falls and the sky turns to night, a fireworks show kicks off outside on the patio terrace, where guests continue to enjoy coffee, dessert and the rest of the evening under the stars. Outside there is something for everyone – quiet areas for conversation, fire pits surrounded by Adirondack chairs, and dancing and live music under the tent with the popular area party band The New York Players.

DeCelle says, "Saratoga National Golf Club provides one of the most elegant and picturesque settings for an event in this area. Since the event begins upstairs in the grand ballroom, then ends outside on the patio terrace, guests are able to enjoy different atmospheres to mingle with their colleagues and friends than at your typical cocktail reception. The setting is a perfect complement to the social summer season that allows our guests to support an important cause."

In 2010, Light up the Night welcomed over 500 guests and raised more than $165,000 in support of the department of emergency medicine at Albany Medical Center. The event also raises awareness for Albany Medical Center in Saratoga County and the strengthening partnership between Albany Medical Center and Saratoga Hospital.

Source: Nicole Stack DeCelle, Associate Director, Signature Events, Albany Medical Center Foundation, Albany, NY. E-mail: StackN@mail.amc.edu

Volunteer Commitment Keeps Event Fresh

Volunteers who commit to year-round support — not just the event itself — help make Light Up the Night a success for the Albany Medical Center Foundation (Albany, NY).

"In the off-season (September–February) our volunteer committee meets every other month to explore new ideas and initiatives to keep our event fresh and exciting, and to begin planning event details and strategies," says Nicole DeCelle, associate director, signature events.

DeCelle says this year-round commitment is especially important, because one of the foundation's biggest challenges in organizing the event is to maintain its uniqueness against a backdrop of so many other charity events and benefits.

"We constantly have to be aware of the timing for the event and come up with new creative ways to make our event stand out from those of other organizations," she says. "One strategy to overcome these challenges is to benchmark against what other successful organizations are doing and what our committee members have seen and heard from other events in the area."

Content not available in this edition

Content not available in this edition

How to Plan Profitable, WOW-Factor Galas

REVENUE: GALA SPONSORSHIPS

Sponsorships can account for a significant amount of your gala's revenue. At a minimum, sponsorships can underwrite your gala's costs; at the most sponsorships can account for the most significant portion of your event's revenue sources. If you're planning a first-time gala, take time to develop a menu of sponsorship opportunities that can be tied to various aspects of your event: overall sponsor, program sponsor, table sponsors, entertainment sponsors, etc. If you're building from an existing event, look for ways to expand sponsorship opportunities and accompanying benefits for would-be sponsors.

Enhance Sponsorship Revenue

Sponsorships — or lack of them — can be the difference between a prospering event and a floundering one. To augment this critical stream of revenue, Jean Block, president of Jean Block Consulting Inc. (Albuquerque, NM), advises event organizers to:

Tip: *To make your gala's sponsors feel even more special, arrange to have them picked up and dropped off at your event in a limousine.*

1. **Seek mission-matched sponsors**. In seeking sponsors, look for businesses that have a natural affinity for your mission, the people you serve or the people who will attend your event. Less-traditional sponsors can be a significant source of untapped potential.

2. **Own the value of your event**. Your event is an important opportunity for sponsors to connect with potential customers, so own that value, says Block. "Businesses are often looking for more impact and visibility. Do some brainstorming, make a list of who would benefit from access to your events and attendees, and approach them with the opportunity to participate."

3. **Rethink sponsorship benefits**. Do your sponsors really care about the banner in the back of the room or the information table in the hallway? Block suggests asking long-time sponsors what benefits they would find most valuable.

4. **Overdeliver on promises**. Numerous nonprofits seek corporate support, so differentiate yourself from the pack by delivering the benefits you promised — and then some, says Block.

5. **Thank each sponsor at least three times**. The first gesture of appreciation should be a handwritten note as soon as a pledge is received. The second should warmly acknowledge the receipt of payment. The third should come after the event, and should enumerate the event's concrete results.

Source: Jean Block, President, Jean Block Consulting Inc., Albuquerque, NM. E-mail: jean@jblockinc.com

Invite Sponsorships Through Your Website

Recruiting area businesses to sponsor an event may be as easy as a click of the mouse.

Morrisville, NC, recently added a new sponsorship page to the town's website (www.townofmorrisville.org/sponsorship). In the first two months of operation, 10 businesses sponsored events in the town of 18,000 people, raising about $10,000. "It seems to be working," says Matt Leaver, the town's recreation superintendent, noting that before the Web page was up only one or two businesses would sponsor events in some years.

In addition to providing information on what events a business can sponsor, the site describes the recognition companies will receive for their sponsorship dollars. Within each category, a business can select its level of sponsorship, ranging from $50 to $3,000. "Each event has a different range of sponsorship levels. It depends what the budget is for each event, how much sponsorship money is needed," says Leaver.

Stephanie Smith, public information officer for Morrisville, is in charge of securing these sponsorships with area businesses. She says many businesses want to sponsor events but don't know how to go about it. "When we first launched the website, we sent a mass postcard mailing to all area businesses with a privilege license from the town, to let them know about the website. This way they could visit the site at their convenience and fill out an online interest form," says Smith.

The online interest form lists all the sponsorship opportunities, so a company can check the box of the event they are interested in sponsoring. The form also asks for the company name, contact person and contact information. It doesn't, however, ask for any dollar amounts.

Both Leaver and Smith agree that having a sponsorship website has helped the town become more efficient and streamlined in its relationship with sponsors. "This way, all sponsors are treated equally," says Leaver.

Sources: Matt Leaver, Recreation Superintendent, Town of Morrisville, Morrisville, NC.
E-mail: mleaver@townofmorrisville.org
Stephanie Smith, Public Information Officer, Town of Morrisville, Morrisville, NC. E-mail: ssmith@townofmorrisville.org

Gala Spotlight ...

Theme, Sponsorship Key to Library Fundraiser

You've probably heard of the bestselling book "Eat, Pray, Love," but how about the fundraising event Eat, Play, Read to benefit a home to books, The Ferguson Library (Stamford, CT)?

"The event was our first ever fundraiser here at the library," says Communications Supervisor Linda Avellar. "We had recently completed a renovation of the main library and wanted to hold the event there, since many people in the community hadn't been in the building since the renovation. The concept Eat, Play, Read was a play on the popular book/film "Eat, Pray, Love," and was meant to be fun and a little whimsical. I think we achieved that with the evening we put together."

A dozen local restaurants and caterers donated food and set up tables to offer tastings. One of the town's major liquor stores donated wine, scotch and beer for tastings, as well as an open bar, reducing event costs tremendously. A jazz band played throughout the evening, while guests enjoyed a live auction and organized tours of the library. Those who participated in the tours were eligible for a raffle at the end of the evening. Avellar says, "It was a great way to get people around the building, and people were thrilled with the tours."

People also enjoyed the fact that the library, an elegant building with soaring ceilings and a grand staircase, was used as the venue.

Avellar says the event's intent was to be both a fundraiser and a friend-raiser. "We hoped to engage the entire Stamford community, especially those who might not be regular library users. We sustained a $1.2 million budget cut this year and were forced to scale back services and reduce hours system wide. Eat, Play, Read was an effort to raise funds and educate the community about what we do. On both accounts, we believe the evening was a big success."

The event raised approximately $100,000. Avellar says they had a robust response from individuals at every level of sponsorship. "We had 38 sponsors total, ranging from $500 to $25,000. The depth of the response was very encouraging." Indeed, it accounted for the majority of revenue raised.

Revenue was also generated through ticket sales, a live auction and a giving tree.

Source: Linda Avellar, Communications Supervisor, The Ferguson Library, Stamford, CT. E-mail: linda@fergusonlibrary.org.

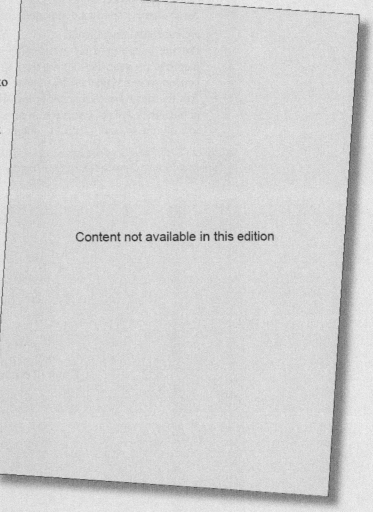

Content not available in this edition

The success of the Eat, Play Read event of The Ferguson Library depended in large part on sponsorship revenue. Shown here is the event-specific sponsorship form organizers used to raise donations of up to $25,000.

Gift Form Streamlines Event Sponsorship Process

The Minneapolis Heart Institute Foundation (Minneapolis, MN) has been hosting To Her Health for three years running to raise awareness to the growing issue of heart disease as the No. 1 killer of women nationwide. Some 250 people attended the four-course wine and dinner event that raised nearly $45,000 for the cause.

One component critical to the event's success is a gift form that event organizers send to potential corporate sponsors prior to the event. The form's purpose is to promote pregiving and secure funds.

"We aim to have between 60 to 75 percent of the projected revenue committed before the invitation hits the mail," says Toni Knorr, donor relations coordinator. "This allows for proper recognition of sponsors, as well as giving a better idea of any changes that might need to be made to the event."

The gift form serves two primary functions — predetermining secured sponsorships and spelling out the way(s) in which sponsors should be recognized at the event.

"The primary purpose of the gift form is for clarification on how a company wants to be recognized, whom to secure guests names from, whom to contact for logo information and more," says Knorr. "All companies completing this form receive communication directly from staff in our office."

Knorr shares important components of an effective gift form:

- Define commitment level.
- Provide an option to pay sponsorship immediately or opt for billing in a specified month of the year. This allows for a sponsor to budget for their sponsorship dollars conveniently within their fiscal year.
- Ask for the preferred manner of identification of the sponsor when listing them in publications and at your event, honoring them for their donation.
- Identify the sponsor contact to obtain logos and attendee names.

Source: Toni Knorr, Donor Relations Coordinator, Minneapolis Heart Institute Foundation, Minneapolis, MN. E-mail: tknorr@mhif.org

Tip: Why wait eight months before re-approaching your current sponsors? Contact existing sponsors within six weeks following the event to report on its success and to re-enlist them for the following year. Also, make next year's benefits (for being a sponsor) even more tantalizing.

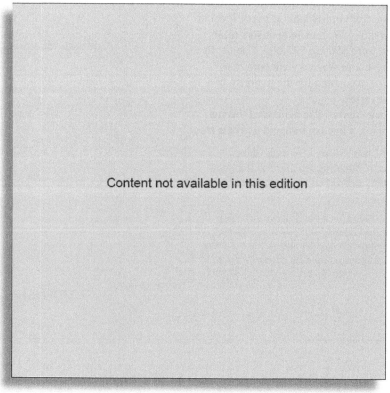

Content not available in this edition

Gala Spotlight ...

Red Shoe Ball Offers Dancing and Donations

Event organizers of the Red Shoe Ball – an annual fundraiser for the Ronald McDonald House (Missoula, MT), understand ruby red slippers are beloved by more than a small girl from Kansas lost in the Land of Oz.

Since 2007, volunteers and organizers of the ball have crafted a highly successful red-shoe-themed event that features dinner, dancing and a live auction. Proceeds from the ball, which takes place at Missoula's Hilton Garden Inn, go toward operating costs for the house — a place of temporary residence for families of pediatric patients seeking medical assistance for their children in Missoula.

One unique, creative element of the ball? All attendees are encouraged (but not required) to wear red shoes.

Art Event Morphs Into Red Shoe Ball

The most recent event, held April 12, 2010, netted $35,000. Revenue sources included sponsorships, donations, auctions, raffle sales, ticket sales and registration costs.

"The first year for a ball benefiting Missoula's Ronald McDonald House was April 2006," says Barbara Wickel, executive director of Missoula's Ronald McDonald House. "The event's theme was Art From the Heart and featured an art auction and the grand opening of Hilton Garden Inn. Hilton has been a major sponsor," she shares. "The event morphed into the Red Shoe Ball the second and third year," she says, explaining that the opportunity to forego black ties and wear red shoes has generated a good deal of interest.

Shoes, Sponsors and a Geek Squad Spell Success

"The event has been successful because of all of the energy and fun related to wearing red shoes — the shoes are a great conversation piece," Wickel says. "In addition, we have very little overhead and have minimal advertising. Our success is also the result of returning sponsors and very loyal patrons."

Wickel shares that the mechanics behind preparing the event included planning nine months in advance and involved 35 volunteers. Participants included specialty volunteers (such as Mrs. Montana, Miss Rodeo Montana and Montana's Junior Miss); area college fraternities and sororities; a volunteer auctioneer and a bank and accounting firm staff, who volunteer to run the registrations and check out. Wickel says Best Buy and the Geek Squad (www.geeksquad.com) are major sponsors each year. As a result, Geek Squad volunteers were available to network all computers, credit card terminals and printers and to troubleshoot at the event.

Adding a Hint of Handmade Mystery

"The last three years also featured theme items to bid on," Wickel says. "There were mystery suitcases, where donors were asked to pack a suitcase representing a mystery location. For instance, an England-themed suitcase may harbor China teacups, tea, a quilt, etc. Italy's themed suitcase might include pasta, a pottery-serving bowl, a travel book, etc. Guests could also bid on hand-painted and decorated children's chairs and handcrafted and donated lamps."

Wickel says that the handcrafted items proved to be a big enough hit to warrant their return for the next event on March 4, 2011. "People appreciate supporting these creative works," she says, as well as the opportunity to create their own favorite pair of red dancing shoes. "Women generally buy their shoes for the event, but men make theirs, often with spray paint, red duct tape, etc."

Source: Barbara Wickel, Executive Director, Ronald McDonald House, Missoula, MT. E-mail: Barbara@rmhmissoula.org

At a Glance —	
Event Type:	Live and silent art auction featuring dinner, dancing
Gross:	$50,000
Costs:	$15,000
Net Income:	$35,000
Volunteers:	35
Planning:	9 months
Attendees:	225
Revenue Sources:	Sponsorships, donations, raffle, auction, tables, dinner registrations ($75/ticket)
Unique Feature:	All attendees encouraged to wear red shoes.

Tried-and-true Event Promotion Techniques Pay Off

Want to boost your event's corporate donations? Easter Seals UCP North Carolina & Virginia (Raleigh, NC) increased corporate donations by 40 percent in the first two years of hosting its Triangle Juice & Jazz event, which mixes wine tasting and live jazz music.

Amy Beros, development manager, offers tips for increasing corporate donations at an event in its infancy:

Tip: To increase the number of event sponsors for your organization and increase existing sponsors' level of support, create a ladder of sponsorship opportunities — higher levels receive more exclusive benefits and greater publicity.

❑ **Coordinate a public service announcement with your partnering radio station.** Offer event tickets for DJs to give away on air and give local radio personalities free tickets. Once you have your DJ's support, they are happy to give on-air promotion.

❑ **Promote the event as a networking vehicle.** By promoting the Juice & Jazz event as a corporate networking event, Beros increased corporate donations by enticing employees of corporations to attend. When you approach a potential sponsor company, know its business and the people its staff may want to meet. Compile a Frequently Asked Questions sheet with statistics of business clientele in attendance from previous years to include with your sponsorship package. "Because of the corporate and high ranking local business people attending, this event is a great networking event, which is how we chose to market to corporate partners," says Beros.

❑ **Provide stewardship opportunities at your event.** The Juice & Jazz event allows Easter Seals UCP staff to provide local corporate partners and its Presidents' Council members complimentary tickets they may distribute freely. "Not only did we receive corporate sponsorship for this event, but most sponsors ended up purchasing additional tickets for more of their staff to attend for the networking benefits and invited their business partners with the allotted complimentary tickets," says Beros.

Source: Amy Beros, Development Manager, Easter Seals UCP, Raleigh, NC.
E-mail: amy.beros@nc.eastersealsucp.com

Recognize Your Event's Corporate Sponsors

You have the good fortune to have a noted corporate sponsor for your next event. Showcasing your partnership helps elevate esteem for both of you. Consider these approaches for involving them in as many high profile ways as possible:

✓ **Name a major service award for the corporation.** If your event includes recognizing key people in your organization, ask the corporate CEO to present the XYZ Company Spirit Award to a top honoree.

✓ **Ask company staff to be judges or announcers.** Your event may have scholarship presentations, prize drawings, an art show with awards or a major auction item. Be sure representatives from the corporation are front and center when all eyes are on that activity.

✓ **Widely use the company logo.** Include the sponsor logo in backdrops, on napkins and nametags, on decorations and in floral arrangements. Athletic events offer opportunities with T-shirts, water bottles or wristbands.

✓ **Ask them to help you identify ways to promote their company.** The direct approach can be the most effective. A brainstorming session with the corporate sponsor's communications staff may uncover some fresh strategies that will come from two distinct viewpoints — theirs and yours.

✓ **Use their facility for your event.** Your sponsor may have wide green lawns, a spacious atrium, an auditorium or dining facility that is ideal for your occasion. More than simply asking that they underwrite food and beverage costs, give them the chance to open their doors and introduce themselves to the community.

✓ **Include them in public service announcements (PSAs).** Ask one of your sponsor's key staff members to make your television or radio PSAs, using an introduction like "Hello, I'm Pat Adams, CEO of XYZ. I hope to see you at the Community Hospital Spring Run for MS awareness. …"

Gala Spotlight ...

Branding, Varied Activities Ensure a Dazzling Event

The annual fundraiser of the Los Gatos Education Foundation (Los Gatos, CA) needed tweaking. While the event was raising money, the confusion attendees seemed to have about proper attire suggested problems with branding and messaging, says Kimberley Ellery, director of special events.

The solution? Denim and Diamonds.

"The theme really established the tone of the evening," Ellery says. "The décor was casual but elegant — red roses and crystal — and the guests looked fabulous. They were very comfortable in their jeans, but outstanding in their jewelry."

Organizers wove the diamond motif throughout the event, from promotional artwork to a jeweler selling diamonds (and donating a portion of the proceeds to the foundation) at the event.

While the theme got people in the door, Ellery credits the variety of activities for securing their support. "We were very deliberate about offering many levels of participation at different price points," says Ellery. "People could jump in for as little as $20, or offer thousands through family sponsorships."

The event's many activities included:

- **Chicken Bingo.** A fenced, 7X7-foot grid of 100 squares was brought to the dance floor and attendees bought individual squares for $20. A diamond-wearing chicken was then placed on the grid, and the owner of the square where it did its business won diamond earrings. Of the event Ellery says, "You could have heard a pin drop in that room, everyone was so fascinated. It was a perfect way to focus attention for the auction."

- **Heads or Tails Raffle.** For $30, participants called successive coin flips until only one remained, winning an iPad tablet computer.

- **Premium Wine Bar.** Guests paid $25 per glass to sample fine wine donated by local vineyards. Five-glass punch cards were available for $100.

- **Best of Raffle.** 100 tickets were sold at $100 each, with the winner receiving his or her choice of any single item offered in the live auction.

- **Wine Toss.** For $15 a toss, attendees attempted to ring the necks of donated bottles of wine. Those who succeeded won the wine and an auction item valued at $50 or less. Ellery says, "It's a great way to get rid of leftover bits that can't be easily packaged or auctioned off, packs of five carwash certificates and things like that."

Other activities including a ticketed Texas Hold 'em tournament, blackjack tables, and live and silent auctions helped the event net $90,000.

Source: Kimberley Ellery, Director of Special Events, Los Gatos Education Foundation, Los Gatos, CA. E-mail: KimberleyEllery@comcast.net

At a Glance —	
Event Type:	Themed Gala
Gross:	$135,000
Costs:	$45,000
Net Income:	$90,000
Volunteers:	6
Planning:	9-12 months
Attendees:	275
Revenue Sources:	Ticket sales, live and silent auctions, blackjack tables, poker tourney, jewelry sales, sponsorships, more
Unique Feature:	Wide variety of activities, price points

Securing Major Corporate Sponsorship

The Denim and Diamonds fundraiser of the Los Gatos Education Foundation (Los Gatos, CA) enjoyed corporate sponsorship from high-profile corporations like OnFulfillment (Newark, CA) and Barracuda Networks (Campbell, CA).

Kimberley Ellery, director of special events, says doing your homework and writing very targeted solicitation letters are critical steps to securing such national-level sponsorships.

"You have to do the research, know exactly what kinds of buckets they donate to and when, and then position yourself firmly in one of those buckets," she says. "Almost all businesses donate somewhere, but most have very strict guidelines about what they do and do not support. So if you want to tap into that level of support, you have to be very clear about how your organization and its event matches their priorities and rules."

How to Plan Profitable, WOW-Factor Galas

PUBLICIZING YOUR GALA, CREATING BUZZ

To maximize attendance and make your gala the talk of the town, use every available opportunity to get the word out about your event and identify specific strategies for creating buzz throughout your community. Part of your efforts should be directed at drawing the public's attention and part should be aimed at grabbing the attention of the media.

Tip: *For a fresh way to promote your event, consider yard signs. They are cheaper than billboards and can be strategically placed in several target areas. Obviously, remember to ask the property owner's permission first.*

Key Tools for Event Publicity

The challenge for small nonprofits and membership organizations, according to Lori Halley, a blogger for Wild Apricot (Toronto, Ontario, Canada), is the need for low-cost event publicity ideas.

Starting early and planning ahead will help small organizations with limited resources publicize their events effectively, says Halley.

Among the tools she mentions for maximizing the benefit of event publicity are:

- **Press Release** — a must-have necessity for drawing attention to your event. Succinctly offering the who, what, where, when, why and how draws media interest and attention to your event.
- **Media Advisory** — a communication inviting the media to attend your event. The advisory should contain the details outlined in your press release and convey a personal welcome extended to members of the media.
- **Media Alert** — a message sent the week prior to the event which reiterates all relevant details one last time.
- **Backgrounder** — a fact sheet with all the event information and pertinent details about your organization. Background information will assist media members in rounding out their coverage of your event.
- **Media Table** — a table at your event where participants and members of the media can find press kits containing the event program, backgrounder, press release, speaker bios, photos and any other collateral materials.

Source: Lori Halley, Wild Apricot Marketing Writer and Blogger, Wild Apricot/Bonasource Inc., Toronto, Ontario, Canada. E-mail: lori@wildapricot.com

Well-crafted Press Releases Maximize Pre-event Publicity

Getting the word out about your special event is one of the most important aspects of the planning process. You may have the greatest event ever, but if no one hears about it, no one will come.

The most cost-efficient way to publicize your event is with a press release to the local media. But while you're sending in your finely crafted press release, so are many other nonprofits.

How do you make your release stand out from all the others to help guarantee it gets published on time and catches the attention of a reporter or assignment editor for a feature story? Here are tips to make sure your press release — and your event — get the attention they deserve:

✓ **Use a style guide.** Some publications use an in-house style guide, but most follow basic rules set forth in guide books such as "The Associated Press Stylebook." If your release is written in the same style as the publication, busy journalists rushing to meet a deadline will not have to rewrite it.

✓ **Write the release to match the purpose.** For the community calendar portion of the newspaper, write in the style of a calendar listing, not a full release. Include only necessary facts. A notice sent to a radio or TV station to be read as a public service announcement (PSA) should also be an abbreviated version of the full release.

✓ **Develop a style sheet of your own.** Having an in-house style sheet helps answer questions such as: What's the correct tag line to describe the organization? Must board member names be included in every release? What phone number or extension should be listed in news stories? Who is the designated press contact? What acronyms need to be explained? It will also give each press release a consistent feel and flair, regardless of who writes it.

Grab the Media's Attention

Looking to gain media attention for your event? You may want coverage in your local newspaper, but wonder where to begin.

Rebecca Leaman, a blogger with Wild Apricot (Toronto, Ontario, Canada), asked two acquaintances — one a longtime editor of a community newspaper and one a freelance reporter — how to make headlines.

Here, Leaman shares their insight into gaining media coverage for your event:

- ❑ **Get familiar with the publication.** Determine what kinds of stories the publication normally runs and if it typically uses press releases or human-interest features about local personalities.
- ❑ **Build a relationship with a reporter or editor.** Check back issues for local stories like yours and note the names of reporters involved. Establishing a relationship with one or two reporters may win you a champion when it comes to pitching stories.
- ❑ **Get to the point of your pitch.** Don't call with a rambling intro to your organization, working toward asking for a story. Instead, ask how to submit an item to the local events calendar or other specific column.
- ❑ **Tell a good story.** Never mind the do-it-yourself public relations advice about reverse pyramid structure and press release formats; hook them with a story that practically writes itself.
- ❑ **Check the editorial calendar.** Does the paper have regular features or seasonal issues that fit with your schedule of activities, events and fundraising campaigns? If so, pitch them!
- ❑ **Put together a media kit.** What can you do to make it easier for the reporter, editor and layout department? Provide press releases, artwork, photographs, logos, and other graphic elements, quotes from key individuals, contacts for more information and other assets that tell your story.

Source: Rebecca Leaman, Wild Apricot Blogger and Jay Moonah, Wild Apricot/Bonasource Inc., Toronto, Ontario, Canada. E-mail: jay@wildapricot.com

Tip: To attract a larger audience to your gala, create a positive buzz.

For example, send an advance notice to all Chamber of Commerce members in your community, enabling them to reserve tickets for your event in advance. Tell those businesses that your event provides an opportunity for them to give a special gift to employees or preferred clients.

Maximize Pre-event Coverage to Boost Event Attendance

Your local newspaper may be agreeable to covering your special event on the day it occurs, but advance publicity that can help boost attendance may be harder to get. Following are several strategies for enlisting their help ahead of time.

- ❑ **Choose before or during.** Since news space and staff time are limited, ask for either advance publicity or event coverage rather than insisting on both. Follow up with one or two great photos of your event and a brief release outlining attendance, funds raised and how they will be used.
- ❑ **Set a realistic but unprecedented goal.** Contact the paper to tell them you hope to boost last year's fundraising total by a record-setting amount. Be sure to mention the local angle of increased community needs for your programs and services.
- ❑ **Let others tell your story.** Ask one or two people who have benefitted from your organization to give interviews about how funds raised from last year's event helped pay for their job training, holiday dinner or back-to-school supplies for their children. Newspapers like inspiring human-interest stories. Make the connection to your event clear by arranging the interviews and providing background.
- ❑ **Invite them to be a sponsor.** Like any business, newspapers seek ways to contribute to their communities. Ask them to become an event sponsor with full benefits, but with a combination of advertising and money. When they promote your event, they will be promoting themselves.
- ❑ **Create an advertising supplement.** Most newspapers have frequent inserts. A sponsor-funded flyer or brochure can be a highly cost-effective way to reach a broad audience.
- ❑ **Cultivate your contacts.** Develop a friendly bond with the staff most likely to cover your organization's events. Send positive notes or e-mails complimenting them on other articles and let them know you take an interest in their section and work in general. Stay in touch even when you don't want something.

Tip: Create an event to promote an event. For example, hold a pre-event hour that gives the public a taste of what's to come. Invite members of the press to be on hand.

Gala Spotlight ...

Opus and Olives Showcases Best-selling Authors

Seven is a lucky number for organizers of Opus & Olives, a special event that benefits The Friends of the Saint Paul Public Library (Saint Paul, MN).

Organizers of the event, which celebrated its seven-year anniversary in 2010, say community participation has doubled since its inception in 2004. The most recent event, held at the Crowne Plaza Riverfront Hotel Saint Paul (Saint Paul, MN), attracted 800 guests and netted $105,000.

Wendy Moylan, the library's director of institutional relations, says the event was inspired by a similar event in Houston, TX.

"We started by seeking co-hosts Pioneer-Press/TwinCities.com," Moylan says. "We were looking for an opportunity to raise awareness of The Friends to new people. We worked with an advisory committee and a board member's design firm in the beginning to develop an event brand that would be unique and have deliberately stuck with it."

Moylan says the event attracts attention because of the opportunity for attendees to spend time with some of America's top authors. The 2010 event featured authors Stanley Trollip, Adriana Trigiani, Joshilyn Jackson, Dave Kindred and Roy Blount Jr.

In addition, Delta Air Lines, an event sponsor, donated two round-trip business-class tickets to Europe, Africa or the Middle East, which drew the attention of 300 people, each of whom paid $100 for a raffle ticket.

The base ticket price for the event was $125. Tables at the event were available at the $1,250; $2,500; and $3,500 levels. Corporate tables started at $2,500. Sponsorships were also available at $5,000; $10,000; $20,000; and $30,000.

Moylan says as guests arrived, they picked up nametags with table assignments. As they approached the reception area, they received a book bag with an event logo.

The authors, whose books were available for purchase at the event, were present as guest speakers and available to sign books and chat before and after dinner.

Moylan credits volunteers for the success of the event.

"Volunteers have been key to defining the scope of the program for each event, as well as the event as a whole," she says. "They recommend authors based on presentation skills and perceived appeal to audience. At the event, they are critical in making people feel welcomed and thanked."

Tremendous support for the event also came from sponsors. Depending upon sponsorship levels, sponsors received exclusive ads and their name and logo on all newspaper ads, print materials and electronic communications, the opportunity to speak from a podium, receive a private reception with the authors and have multiple tables of guests with the author(s) sitting with their guests at dinner.

Moylan says for future events, she would limit the time speakers are allowed to talk.

"Each year we struggle with trying to control our speakers," she says. "On average, one each year will talk too long, which disrupts the flow and spirit of the event. We will look at means to cut a speaker off without being disrespectful, because our responsibility is to our guests."

But despite the occasional verbosity of a speaker, Moylan says overall the event was an achievement.

"The venue was filled to capacity, people consistently say they love this event and profits continue to increase," she says. "Year after year, we find that our friends bring their friends, who then become our friends. So while event profits increase, we also have attracted new board members, as well as individual and corporate gifts due to connections made at the event."

Source: Wendy Moylan, Director of Institutional Relations, The Friends of the Saint Paul Public Library, Saint Paul, MN.

At a Glance —

Event Type:	Dinner with multiple speakers
Gross:	$205,000
Costs:	$100,000
Net Income:	$105,000
Volunteers:	20
Planning:	10 months
Attendees:	800
Revenue Sources:	Ticket sales, raffle, corporate sponsorship, book sales
Unique Feature:	Nationally known authors visit with guests and speak at event

How to Plan Profitable, WOW-Factor Galas

Promote Your Event Online

As nonprofits continue to expand their reach through online resources, it makes sense that websites that help promote events would create opportunities for nonprofits to access their services.

Here is what you need to know about these three major event-promotion websites:

- **Eventbrite** (www.eventbrite.com) lets nonprofits create a customizable event page, spread the word through social media, collect money and gain visibility. Events that are free to attend are listed at no charge. Events with entrance fees can be listed for a fee (2.5 percent plus $0.99 per ticket or payment processing using credit cards, PayPal, or Google Checkout for no more than 3 percent of ticket price). Eventbrite also offers Eventbrite for Causes, a special component of services and resources just for nonprofits.

- **Eventful** (www.eventful.com) offers a free component and paid upgrade. The free component lets organizations post events and add venues to the website. Upgrading allows promotion through its weekly events guide e-newsletter.

- **Zvents** (www.zvents.com), according to its website, lets people "discover and choose fun things to do." Basic listings are free, with premium listings that include images, videos and links to tickets starting at $19.95.

Attendance-busting Ideas

To increase attendance for your event, find a way to get on the evening news the week of your event. To do that, come up with an attention-grabbing hook that local stations will want to carry.

Consider any of these ideas:

✓ Showcase a handful of individuals who will benefit from the funds being raised.

✓ If it's a themed event, enlist two or three people to be interviewed in costume.

✓ Share the name(s) of any celebrities who will be in attendance.

✓ Announce the chance for any attendees to win a major prize.

Spark Interest in Attractions With Past Event Photos

Your winter gala was the talk of the town last year with spectacular food, decorations and entertainment — and you have the photos to prove it.

Why not use some of the best photos to promote or generate interest in your upcoming party?

Here are some creative ways in which to incorporate those photographs.

- **Create save-the-date postcard.** Use one terrific, colorful photo or a sampling of fun pictures on the front of your save-the-date card with the message, "Don't miss the fun this year!"

- **Use them as background on print ads.** A panoramic shot of your event venue filled with happy crowds and festive decorations from last year can give potential guests a great visual image of themselves attending this year's party and send the message, "This is the place to be on February 22nd."

- **Make a large photo puzzle.** Choose your best crowd shot and create a gigantic puzzle to be cut into a reasonable number of pieces (250, 500). Include them as teasers in your invitations, asking guests to bring their unique piece to the event to build the compete puzzle.

- **Hold an online caption contest.** It's not unusual to post event photos on your website, but asking for amusing caption contributions for some of the most entertaining can add fun while promoting the next occasion. Offer prizes in various categories the night of the event.

- **Set up a slide show** in your building's lobby a few weeks ahead of time. Interested visitors can enjoy the show, pick up ticket information, make reservations, volunteer for a committee or even make a donation.

- **Make a Facebook album and event page.** Facebook has become one of the most affordable and efficient vehicles for publicizing special events. You can combine a large photo album with the RSVP interface to get a reasonable idea of potential attendance. Even those who don't attend may enjoy seeing pictures of their friends and will learn more about your cause.

Tip: Ever notice that the most well-attended, popular events are the ones that people are talking about weeks ahead of time?

Get the word out. If you can get the public talking about your event in advance, it's well on its way to becoming a big hit.

Gala Spotlight ...

Black Tie Optional, Hiking Boots Mandatory for Ball

When planning your next event, get creative to host a special event that celebrates your organization's mission while providing a fresh, fun opportunity for attendees.

Adirondack Mountain Club's (Lake George, NY) director of membership & development, Deborah Zack, had an idea buzzing around in her head for years — a formal affair celebrating persons who are active hikers and paddlers, but who also enjoy dancing and the opportunity to socialize.

The idea became a reality in 2009 at the club's first Black Fly Affair: A Hiker's Ball, which raised more than $43,500 for the organization.

What made the event such a success the first time out? One factor that Zack says people really picked up on was the unique dress theme, Black Tie Optional — Hiking Boots Mandatory.

The 350 guests took the theme and ran with it, she says. "Some came dressed in tuxes and formal gowns, some in cocktail dresses and some in kilts. One man even came in khakis with a piece of black tape covering his fly. But every one of them was in hiking boots!"

To boost interest and carry on the creative theme, Zack says, they carried the concept through on the marketing materials, as well. Zack and her designer added hiking boots to an image of dancing silhouettes. They also used boot prints and dance steps in the invitations mailed to 5,000 members and donors.

To garner further attention, Zack and her team marketed it using their member magazine, which reaches 20,000 households, on the organization's website, and in newspaper print ads, online calendars, local public radio spots and flyers. They sent press releases to regional media outlets.

Another selling point was the event location — in the Adirondack mountains at a site overlooking beautiful Lake George. Guests enjoyed a wine tasting from a local winery and ale tastings from a local brew master, along with a chocolate fondue fountain and several food stations. The evening was rounded out with silent and live auctions, and dancing to favorites from the 1940s, '50s '60s and '70s, including fox trots, Lindy hops, cha-chas, swing and rock and roll.

To generate excitement for the second annual event, held May 21, 2010, organizers featured online registration on the front page of the organization's website (www.adk.org) that showed the silhouette images of the hiking boot-wearing dancing couple and the phrase, "Be part of the buzz — no, *be* the buzz!" Attendees paid $45 a ticket with the option of making an additional tax-deductible contribution to benefit the nonprofit club.

Source: Deborah Zack, Director, Membership & Development, Adirondack Mountain Club, Lake George, NY. E-mail: deb@adk.org

---

What Happens After Event is Key to Its Ongoing Success

It's no secret that events are immensely labor-intensive. That's why Deborah Zack, director, membership & development, Adirondack Mountain Club (Lake George, NY) says the most important part of any event is what happens after it's over:

"Having a good cultivation plan is key. Think about what you want to get out of the event. People have many ways of supporting your organization. Ask how the event-goers wish to get more involved and think about how you can get them more involved."

How to Plan Profitable, WOW-Factor Galas

REVENUE: MAXIMIZING ATTENDANCE, TICKET SALES

How many guests do you hope to attract? Is there a limit on the number of guests that can attend? Is there a particular group of people you want to attract? Have a plan in place to maximize your gala's attendance and get your board members and volunteers to assume ownership for getting people to participate.

Aim for High Attendance

If the success of your event depends, for the most part, on a minimum number of paying guests, you will want to do whatever is possible to maximize attendance.

Follow these steps to help ensure you reach those attendance numbers:

1. **Build event ownership among as many people as possible early on in the process.** If they own it, they will come. Get people personally connected to the event's success and not only will they attend, they will help get others there, too. That's why the most successful events have several types of committees with large numbers of volunteers involved.

2. **Appoint a committee to sell tickets and get people to attend.** Be sure they know and accept that expectation before they agree to help. Offer inexpensive incentives for selling a set number of tickets.

3. **Make it attractive to buy multiple tickets.** Some events that include a meal, for instance, offer guests the opportunity to purchase an entire table of eight or 10. A golfing event might promote funding a foursome of golfers in addition to the individual option.

Three Ways to Get Last Year's Attendees Back Again

It's been proven time and again: It's much easier to retain an existing customer or client than it is to recruit a new one. For that reason alone, it's important to retain your special event attendees from year to year, particularly if you want to grow attendance over time.

That being said, here are three ways to get last year's attendees back again:

1. **Evaluate their perceptions.** Don't hesitate to get attendees' opinions on what they liked and didn't like about your event. Survey them and/or talk to them within five days of the event, while everything is fresh in their minds. Pay as much attention to what guests enjoyed as you do their negative perceptions.

2. **Give past attendees first choice at subsequent years' events.** Send out your first round of invitations to last year's attendees, giving them top seating, best parking, first choice at seeing auction items and so forth. By distinguishing this loyal group from others, future first-time guests will also want to become part of this elite group.

3. **Recognize past attendees.** Include names of all ticket purchasers in your printed program. (You will, no doubt, need a cutoff date for printing purposes; however, this could even be a program insert prepared at the last minute.) Beside each name, include the number of years the individual has attended your special event. Also, you could ask all previous event attendees to stand and be recognized during the program.

Create a Plan to Beat Last Year's Attendance

If you repeat a particular fundraising event each year, how much time do you put into setting attendance goals designed to surpass the previous years' numbers? That key aspect of your event deserves a written plan.

Some of the components of that plan may include:

Making every effort to get previous guests to attend —

- Offer special perks to anyone who attended last year's event — special seating or parking or an opportunity to attend a preview of the event.

- Get last year's attendees signed up before anyone else (e.g. early bird invitation).

Pursuing specific strategies aimed at attracting new attendees —

- Get previous years' attendees involved in inviting friends and associates to this year's event.

- Add new features to your event that may attract those who had no previous interest (e.g., special entertainment, a celebrity, a one-of-a-kind auction item).

Set an attendance goal for your next event and back up the increase with specific strategies aimed at meeting that goal.

Steps for Boosting Ticket Sales

The financial success of a special event is often based on ticket sales. That's why it's so important that everyone involved takes responsibility for getting tickets sold. This is especially true if you are relying on volunteers for significant ticket sales.

To boost ticket sale success — and ultimately the success of your event:

- Plan backwards: The amount of revenue you want to generate will dictate both number of tickets you need to sell and ticket price. From there you can determine number of ticket sellers needed and minimum number of tickets each volunteer will need to sell.

- Get everyone involved in planning the event — not just those on the ticket committee — to agree to a minimum number of ticket sales.

- Agree that if volunteers cannot sell the agreed-to minimum ticket number, they will be responsible for buying the tickets they hold. (If you're confident this measure will pass, take a vote on it to make it more official.)

- Use the pyramid method of selling: A certain number of captains are responsible, in turn, for enlisting a minimum number of ticket sellers.

- Make it appealing for attendees to purchase a group of tickets (e.g., table of eight). Provide corresponding benefits for those who purchase a group/table of tickets — preferred seating, special favors, recognition, etc.

- Use friendly competition to encourage ticket sales. Offer an incentive, for instance, to any who sell a certain number of tickets by a particular date.

- For an annual event, allow veteran volunteers the privilege of selling tickets to those who have purchased from them in previous years.

- Provide event sponsors with a limited number of tickets for their employees as a perk.

How to Increase Ticket Sales by 30 Percent

Tips for Getting Tickets Sold

To encourage all event planners to sell advance tickets, offer a motivational incentive — a priceless item — based on meeting an established quota and deadline. Such items might include:

1. Special parking privileges for a set period of time.

2. An invitation to an exclusive get-together — perhaps a pre-reception with your event's celebrity.

3. Special seating.

4. Recognition during the event — special name badges, standing to be recognized.

5. Not having to assist with some element of the event (e.g., cleanup).

6. A celebrity-autographed item.

7. Special membership privileges enjoyed by others who give at higher levels.

If your goal is to raise more money with your special event, you can either raise the ticket price or attract more guests. Either way, you need to make sure tickets get sold.

Begin by doing the math. Assuming your ticket price is set, let's say you want to increase ticket sales by 30 percent over last year. If 200 people attended last year's event, that's 60 more tickets that need to be sold.

Knowing board members and volunteers play a key role in selling tickets, consider any of these strategies as a way to boost ticket sales significantly:

- Ask 50 of the previous year's most loyal attendees to each sell two tickets.

- Offer donated prizes (Netbook, iPod, restaurant gift certificate) for most tickets sold.

- Offer a lesser prize (signed book, Starbucks gift cards) to anyone who sells a minimum number of tickets.

- Extend an invitation for your employees to sell tickets and attend the event for free or at a reduced rate as a way to thank them.

Gala Spotlight ...

Event Draws on Popularity of TV Show, Celebrity Dancers

Attendees of a special benefit for the Boys and Girls Club of Sunnyside and Woodside (Sunnyside, NY) were swept away by an evening of artful dance and dining in November 2010.

Modeled after the popular "Dancing With the Stars" ABC television program, the event held at St. Rafael's gymnasium in Long Island City, NY, raised funds for Boys and Girls Club programs within the community as well as for the long-term goal of building a community center.

Organized by volunteer Vincent Renda, a financial advisor with Edward Jones (Sunnyside, NY), and a team of more than 20 volunteers, the event featured 10 professional dancers teamed with 10 celebrities from the community, including teachers, coaches and community activists.

More than 230 people attended the event, which gained a net income of $14,000.

The Sunnyside event attracted the contributions of City Councilman Jimmy Van Bramer, who pledged to follow up the $5,000 donation his office made in 2010 with a donation of at least that much in 2011. "Van Bramer is a big part of our community," Renda says. "So, I just sat down with him and explained to him the situation in our community and he felt inspired. … He felt there is a huge need for the youth in our community. He just requested that we (submit) the proper paperwork to get grant money from the city council, so that is why he pledged the money he did."

Other revenue sources came from admission, raffles, and sales of ads for a journal distributed at the event that featured biographies of the dancers. Some 25 local businesses placed ads, which cost $100 per page.

Renda says they strongly encouraged buying tickets in advance to know how much food to order and beverages to provide. They lowered costs by having local beer distributors donate beer; liquor distributors also donated 72 bottles of wine, which significantly lowered costs. Local restaurants also offered discounts on food they catered for the food service, Renda says. "These are all great opportunities for businesses to show how much they do for our community."

Renda says they featured dance judges solely for entertainment value. People in the audience voted on the couple they wished to win by donating dollars in buckets circulated by local scouts.

Volunteer couples received a month of free lessons from professional dancers prior to their performance, he says. "We also encouraged these couples to bring their friends and family. We had one star who brought almost 40 people just to see this person perform and see how much about dancing they could learn in a month. People were excited to see a great show and also to help out in raising money for our cause."

Source: Vincent Renda, Financial Advisor, Edward Jones, Sunnyside, NY

At a Glance —	
Event Type:	Dancing competition
Gross:	$30,000
Costs:	$16,000
Net Income:	$14,000
Volunteers:	50
Planning:	3 months
Attendees:	232
Revenue Sources:	Contributions, ticket sales, raffles, sales of event journal ads, donated votes
Unique Feature:	Professional dancers team with local celebrities

Event Organizer Pledges to Sell Raffle Tickets Earlier Next Time

Vincent Renda, organizer of the celebrity dancing benefit for the Boys and Girls Club of Sunnyside and Woodside (Sunnyside, NY), says one lesson he learned is to start selling raffle tickets earlier next time around.

For the November 2010 event, he says, they had a goal of selling 500 raffle tickets at $100 each, but sold just 260. The raffle tickets were for a chance at one of four cash prizes: $10,000, $7,000, $5,000 and $3,000, for a total payout of $25,000.

Had they sold all 500 tickets, he says, they would have netted $25,000. Instead, they netted just $1,000 on this portion of the event.

"We didn't sell as many raffle tickets as we should have and it was mainly because of the short time period that we began planning for it," Renda says. "Maybe if we would have had a little more time besides three months and started in advance to sell the raffles, we would have had significantly more money."

Five Steps to Engage the Wealthy in Your Event

Every organization enjoys having a base of wealthy supporters, but too often these important persons make generous contributions without attending fundraising events.

Take steps to change that, realizing that the presence of these key supporters at your special events helps to publicly convey the message that your mission is important and worth others' support.

Employ these strategies to attract persons of wealth — and their friends — to your next gala.

1. **Ask them to host a table.** As most people do, many wealthy people enjoy a bargain or having someone else occasionally offer to pick up the tab. Give these key players two complimentary tickets for hosting a group of eight to 10 attendees who pay full price.

2. **Recognize their contributions.** Awards of appreciation for support can help ensure that not only the individual, but also his or her friends and family will attend the event to be present for the recognition.

3. **Tell them their presence is crucial and meaningful.** Be direct. Tell the persons whom you most want to attend your function that they do indeed make a difference because of their standing and respect in the community. Note specific examples for each person, explaining that potential supporters who admire the individuals and their actions may be moved to become active in your organization.

4. **Play down the glitz factor.** While your event may be the community's over-the-top gala of the year, that may also be the reason some very wealthy people send money but skip the party. Encourage them to attend to meet newcomers who have become involved since they last attended a major function, and to see old friends.

5. **Target them for specific events.** Does the folksy but reclusive millionaire who sends quarterly contributions fit in best at a black-tie dinner or a down-home barbecue? Instead of hoping he will simply show up at both, personally ask him to come to the event that will be the most fun. Ask for his suggestions for entertainment.

Offer Higher-priced Tickets

When planning a special event, consider offering a ticket priced higher than that of other guests that includes exclusive benefits for anyone willing to pay the higher price.

Examples of benefits might include:

- Photo taken with a celebrity speaker.
- Invitation to a pre- or post-event reception.
- Special parking, seating.
- A book autographed by your celebrity author.
- Additional menu or refreshment choices.

Promote Notable Guests

If a notable person within your community RSVPs to your annual event invitation, why not use that as leverage to entice other prominent guests?

Acquiring a Who's Who guest list can help draw larger attendance at your primary events. Try the following tips to creating a Who's Who event:

- Prior to sending out your mass invitation list, secure notables from your community to attend your event. Personally invite the mayor, area celebrities and prominent professionals to attend. When these notables agree to attend, ask to use their names to promote the event.

- Create a Notable Guests or Who's Who section on your mass invitations, e-invites, website and publicity materials that offers a list of prominent guests and a brief quote from each individual about your organization and why they wish to attend.

- Create color-coded nametags for notable guests to wear at the event so others may seek them out (get their approval before doing so).

- Ask a notable guest or two to speak on behalf of your organization the night of the event for an added special touch.

Gala Spotlight ...

Unique Food and Drink Pairings Create Party in Guests' Mouths

Get people raving about your food and drink and you'll have a successful event on your hands. Just ask Stacy LaCombe-Kraft, coordinator of special events and gifts at Seton Health Foundation (Troy, NY), where amazing food and decadent drinks are the rule for the annual Hopscotch & Slide fundraiser.

"Guests are not just eating and drinking," she says, "they are experiencing. When people attend, we want them to be exposed to new and exciting food and drink partnerships that essentially create a party in your mouth."

To accomplish this, organizers place stations throughout the room that pair a culinary style with a specific beverage type (Hops, Scotch, Martini Slide and wine). For example, says LaCombe-Kraft, "This year Mansion Catering featured Asian delicacies like Japanese dim sum and sesame Thai chicken skewers with the Martini Slide station. The Absolute Berri Acai martinis were served from an ice sculpture with a built-in luge and the station was decorated like an Asian pagoda."

LaCombe-Kraft says the high-energy atmosphere also appeals to the younger professional crowd they seek to target. They achieve this by immediately surrounding guests with elements that appeal to all of the senses. This year that meant guests stepping off elevators at the venue onto a Hollywood-style red carpet complete with a paparazzi-style photo shoot.

Unique Pairings Also Boost Silent Auction

Stacy LaCombe-Kraft, coordinator of special events and gifts, Seton Health Foundation (Troy, NY) says their annual Hopscotch & Slide event not only benefits from unique pairings of food and signature drinks, but from strategic pairing of auction items as well.

"We spend weeks packaging items together, rearranging, creating bid sheets and inventing attractive displays," she says. "We also pay attention to feedback from guests and do our best to obtain donations that will enhance the packages and appeal to bidders."

The silent auction, which is a significant part of the fundraising evening, typically has more than 50 items, including big-ticket items such as packages with concert tickets and sports memorabilia.

LaCombe-Kraft says the auction is set up in categories so people can stick to the most appealing items, like date night packages which pair restaurants, hotels and show tickets together. This year's big sellers included a flat screen TV and Rock Band Hero combo package, as well as a trip to see "Wicked" on Broadway and an autographed Mickey Mantle photograph.

LaCombe-Kraft says the event's success still comes down to having an exceptional event planning committee to help you gain momentum. "Hopscotch & Slide would never happen if we didn't have an incredible team of hand-picked individuals who understand the experience we are trying to create as well as the importance of the cause. Our committee members believe in the Seton Health mission and are dedicated to improving the event year after year so that we are constantly out-doing ourselves."

The event has raised more than $360,000 to benefit Seton Health Pediatrics since 2002 and celebrated its 10th anniversary in 2011.

Source: Stacy LaCombe-Kraft, Coordinator of Special Events and Gifts, Seton Health Foundation, Troy, NY. E-mail: SLacombe@setonhealth.org

How to Plan Profitable, WOW-Factor Galas

Preview Parties Add to Events' Success

Many nonprofits plan preview parties as part of their signature events to attract a new demographic, increase revenue and renew media interest.

One such organization is the Siskin Children's Institute (Chattanooga, TN), a nonprofit that offers education, outreach and healthcare to children with special needs and their families. The institute is marking the 35th year of its signature fundraising event, StyleWorks, as well as the third year of the event's preview party, ArtWorks.

"ArtWorks contributed approximately 16 percent to the bottom line in 2010, which is an increase from the first year and a trend that we expect to continue," says Jasmin Rippon, special events coordinator.

To encourage persons to attend both the preview party and main event, Rippon says, they seek to make the companion events similar yet different. StyleWorks, for example, consists of an artists' marketplace followed by a sit-down luncheon and runway show. ArtWorks offers the same marketplace-like shopping experience with the addition of a silent art auction and more of a cocktail-party feel. ArtWorks' cocktail party, Rippon says, "attracts many young professionals whom we'd like to cultivate into future donors, and more men attend ArtWorks since it's a more gender-neutral event."

Preview parties are typically presented the night before the main event in the same venue, or in one section of that venue. For the Siskin Institute, Rippon says, this too leads to greater ticket sales and a more diverse attendance. Because ArtWorks is held on a Friday night, "it is a way to attract guests who could not come to StyleWorks."

Planning the events back-to-back streamlines planning and preparation and allows attendees of one event to feel like they're getting a taste of the other, she says.

While some organizations may limit preview party attendance to VIPs or major donors, Rippon says they open ArtWorks to the public to draw in more potential supporters. However, "For our higher-level StyleWorks ticket holders and sponsors, the ArtWorks tickets are included in their packages." Otherwise, ArtWorks tickets are $25 per person on their own or $10 if purchased with a StyleWorks ticket.

"When ArtWorks was introduced, it was planned as a separate event," Rippon says. "After the first year, we realized that to help the event grow, it made sense to combine the planning processes. We now treat ArtWorks as a subcommittee of StyleWorks, with the chair of ArtWorks sitting on the StyleWorks steering committee."

To further promote the events as similar yet different, organizers create similar-sounding slogans in branding and promoting them as partner events. StyleWorks' slogan is "Fashion With Compassion," while ArtWorks' is "Art With Heart," says Deborah Luehrs, director of marketing and communications. "The names work well together, they're easy to remember, and the short taglines get the point across quickly."

Sources: Deborah Luehrs, Director of Marketing and Communications; Jasmin Rippon, Special Events Coordinator, Siskin Children's Institute, Chattanooga, TN.
E-mail: deborah.luehrs@siskin.org or jasmin.rippon@siskin.org

---

Reach Out to Growing Areas of Your Community

Is your community becoming more culturally diverse? If so, are you stepping up PR methods accordingly? Say that your community has growing numbers of Hispanics and Asians. Bring in representatives of such communities at all stages of event planning — from coming up with ideas that would appeal to persons of other cultures, to helping reach other cultures through newspapers, churches, social groups and other means.

Gala Spotlight ...

Breakfast Galas Boost Fundraising, Recruitment Efforts

Prospective donors and volunteers have a deluge of gala dinners, walkathons, auctions and similar events to choose from when deciding where to give their time, money and attention.

To stand out from that pack, consider organizing a breakfast gala.

When staff of the Capital Breast Care Center (CBCC), a community health center in Washington, D.C., began brainstorming its first-ever large fundraising event, "We opted not to go with an evening event, because in my opinion there are just so many of them," says Beth Beck, executive director. "Very few do breakfast events, so we could be unique in that way."

The CBCC's annual breakfast gala raised $50,000 the first year and $100,000 in both its second and third years.

Punch Up Pledge Card Power

Look for multiple ways to share your message and your need with your event attendees.

At the annual breakfast gala for the Capital Breast Care Center (CBCC), Washington, D.C., for example, in addition to watching a moving video to encourage increased donations, attendees receive pledge cards that detail different ask amounts, and what each amount will provide at the center. For example, next to the box a donor would check if he/she was pledging $50 is the statement: "$50 will provide one woman with her annual mammogram."

Helping donors visualize how their money will be allocated — and how it will directly impact another person's life for the better — is a powerful way to increase donations and, ultimately, awareness of the good your cause does.

In addition to being a unique event to put on one's social calendar, there are two additional ways that a breakfast gala may be a better choice than other types of fundraising events, Beck says:

❏ **Guaranteed time commitment for guests.** As opposed to dinner receptions — which have the reputation of going on too long because of entertainment or an overextended cocktail hour — a breakfast gala, by its very nature, will be run on a tight schedule. It promotes a warm yet get-down-to-business ambience, Beck says. The CBCC's breakfast gala lasts exactly one hour. Because it sticks to its schedule, attendees are pleased with the event and are more likely to return the following year, bringing along more of their friends, family and community members as prospective donors. Beck says attendance at the CBCC's breakfast has increased each year by about 100 people.

❏ **Guaranteed time period for programming.** Because the event does not run over schedule, the event leaders hold the attention of the attendees throughout the program. Therefore, when the CBCC plans its breakfast, it can build up attention over the course of the hour, rather than worry about losing people's attention. "Right before our ask at the end of the event, we show a video in which a woman speaks about the care she received at the center. It creates a personal connection and allows people to really understand what the center does. Even though the video comes at the end of the event, it is the most powerful moment."

Beth Beck, Executive Director, Capital Breast Care Center, Washington, D.C.
E-mail: info@capitalbreastcare.org

How to Plan Profitable, WOW-Factor Galas

REVENUE: MAKING THE MOST OF LIVE, SILENT AUCTIONS

Auctions, both silent and live, can account for a major portion of a gala's revenue. What you intend to "sell" and how you present those items will impact guests' level of participation in the auctions. And there are several auction strategies you can use to make these experiences far more successful.

Host Gift-gathering Party for Your Special Event

Looking for a way to get a wide variety of auction items without tapping out your resources? Host a gift-gathering party.

Laura Henry, director of alumni & events, Bishop Machebeuf High School (Denver, CO), says they get more than half their auction items this way, holding several of these events per year.

For the gift-giving parties, Henry says, "We create a fun opportunity for our current school families and alumni, and their admittance into the event is an auction item to benefit our spring gala."

The school holds a spa day for women where admission is an auction item, and a poker party for men, in which their admittance is a gift of sports memorabilia, tickets or man-pleasing items such as tools and oil changes.

Admission to a wine-tasting event is gained by gifting a bottle of wine valued at $20 or more. Henry says they use the bottles to create a wine cellar that is auctioned off during the live auction portion of the gala, typically garnering more than $1,200.

In addition to being a boon for their gala auction, the gift-gathering events boost morale for the school while fostering friendships. "Our parents love this program," says Henry. "It is a great opportunity to have social functions off campus while giving back to the school."

Source: Laura Henry, Director of Alumni & Events, Bishop Machebeuf High School, Denver, CO.
E-mail: lhenry@machebeuf.org

Think Creatively When Seeking Live Auction Items

The nonprofit Volunteers Enlisted to Assist People (VEAP) of Bloomington, MN, will hold its 12th annual VEAP Holiday Benefit this year.

The event draws about 400 to 450 guests and is the largest fundraiser for the nonprofit, which raised $144,000 last year. The organization has set its sights on this year's goal to raise $200,000 from ticket sales, silent and live auction sales, sponsorship and in-kind donations.

"We actively seek family and business sponsorships, control costs by seeking in-kind sponsors, offer a fun live auction, a large silent auction, and at the end of our program we raise money with a fund-in-need ask to end the evening," says Sharon Paulson, events coordinator for VEAP.

VEAP event organizers pride themselves on obtaining unique and creative live auction items which will bring top dollar.

To obtain the most creative live auction items for your next fundraiser, Paulson suggests holding frequent brainstorming sessions with creative thinkers within your organization, looking within your organization for resources. She also suggests not being afraid to ask for any over-the-top donation.

Paulson offers a few useful tips and ideas to consider when developing your list of live auction items:

- **Be creative**. VEAP explores all avenues for items, and this year will feature a couple of wonderfully themed meals prepared by two area chefs who are committed to sharing their gifts for VEAP's cause.
- **Think outside the box**. VEAP event organizers asked entertainer Mick Sterling, VEAP's special guest performer, to donate his music for a house party live auction item.
- **Think big**. VEAP is orchestrating a vacation with a flight for two donated by Southwest Airlines.
- **Attract all attendees**. VEAP's live auction will likely include a sports package featuring local professional teams.

Source: Sharon Paulson, Events Coordinator, Volunteers Enlisted to Assist People, Bloomington, MN.
E-mail: sharonp@veapvolunteers.com

Silent Auctions Are Easy and Profitable

A silent auction can add spark and profits to your event. Even if you have no experience with this activity, you can be successful. Try these tips:

Acquire auction items through various means:

- Solicit donations from businesses and offer publicity in return.
- Buy additional auction items on sale and add value by packaging them with other items.
- Collect gift certificates for services (e.g., house cleaning, pet sitting).
- Inspire competition among those soliciting items with a contest for best gift package.

Dress up your auction items:

- Keep in mind that eye candy is the byword at silent auctions. Visually desirable displays draw higher bids.
- Bundle related items (bubble bath, candles, lotion) in stunning baskets.
- Accessorize small pieces. Display jewelry in a crystal box on a silk scarf.
- Exhibit gift certificates, such as a spa visit, on quality embroidered towels.

Think through the bidding process in advance:

- Prepare a bid sheet detailing the offering (e.g., limo ride and dinner for two at Captain Jack's).
- For public bidding, have participants record their name/number and the dollar amount bid on bid sheets next to each item, allowing guests to view the earlier bids.
- For anonymity, assign guests a bid number, or have them place their name and top bid on a slip of paper deposited in a container.
- At a set time, announce the winning bidder of each item.

Inspire Additional Auction Gifts

Reward the biggest spender — Announce that the person who spends the most on silent auction purchases will earn a private dinner with your board chair and agency's CEO.

Stimulate competition and spending — A contest for most attractive basket or best silent auction display can bring additional donations. Place a secure container or assign a volunteer to each basket. Each dollar placed in the container counts as a vote. At event end, count the dollars and honor the winning entry.

Make it easy to spend money — Let attendees know in advance that you accept credit cards to encourage higher bids.

Successful Auction Strategies

With 17 years as a licensed auctioneer and a nonprofit client list that includes Make-A-Wish Foundation, the American Heart Association and more major names, Dawn Rose-Sohnly knows what it takes to make a nonprofit fundraising auction a success.

President and owner of Elite Consulting LLC (Maumee, OH), she shares some of her best advice for auction success:

- ❑ **Establish a contract and understand the legalities related to the event.** The contract should outline responsibilities of the auctioneer; bid assistants; who is collecting the money raised; whether the auctioneer is licensed and bonded; and who is providing the clerks, cashiers, and any other additional help at the auction. Be aware of your state's auction laws, as well as sales tax and license laws.
- ❑ **Provide Internet bidding.**
- ❑ **Plan ahead how minimum bids will be handled.**
- ❑ **Hire a professional auctioneer.** An experienced auctioneer knows the bid increment levels, knows how to encourage bidding and knows how to communicate with the audience.
- ❑ **Understand your audience.** If you're asking for $5,000 for a specific item, know you have someone in the room who will contribute that amount.
- ❑ **Use bid assistants/bid spotters** to help create excitement, encourage bidding, establish rapport and expedite the sale of items being sold.
- ❑ **Understand the auction software.** Make sure whoever is working with the software is familiar with it inside and out. If you do not have the auctioneer collect the funds raised, consider hiring a company such as Auction Pay to keep the checkout line moving.
- ❑ **End with a follow-up meeting.** Do so one week after the auction to discuss aspects that worked well, and those that need more attention.

Source: Dawn Rose-Sohnly, President & Owner, Elite Consulting LLC, Whitehouse, OH.
E-mail: dawn@elitebenefitauctions.com.

Gala Spotlight ...

Firefighters Give Their All for Charity Auction

A live auction is at the heart of the annual fundraiser for the Idaho Federation of Families for Children's Mental Health (Boise, ID).

But this isn't your typical auction.

Up for bid? Fifteen tuxedo-wearing bachelors.

And these aren't your typical bachelors.

The well-dressed gentlemen up for bid include firefighters from area departments, smoke jumpers and members of hotshot crews, all part of the organization's live auction packages.

"Each fireman is an individual volunteer and not required to participate through his fire department or crew," says Lacey Sinn, development director.

How does she find participants?

"I have always recruited through personal contacts and have then moved to visiting individual fire departments, contacting local fire department chiefs for support," Sinn says. "And now that our event has taken place for three years, I also contact previous bachelors for recruiting suggestions. We have also had individual firemen contact us and offer to volunteer."

Bachelors are paired with an auction package that includes dinner for two and a local activity such as a movie, rock climbing, a magic show or outdoor concert.

For the 2009 event, bachelors and date packages were auctioned for $75 to $800, bringing in a total of $5,250. Bringing in an additional $3,510 were ticket sales — $25 in advance and $30 at the door. Admission included hors d'oeuvres, a hosted bar, professional photos with the bachelors and an after-party with a live band.

If your organization is interested in hosting a bachelor auction, Sinn offers the following suggestions:

- Begin planning early.

- Solicit a well-known emcee. "We were lucky to have a local radio personality who has donated her time to the event as an emcee the last three years," Sinn says. "I would encourage anyone looking to do a similar event to search out someone like that. Not only did it give us a great emcee for our event, but it also gave us a lot of free promotion."

- Hire a professional auctioneer.

- Choose a location that permits outside catering. "If it is at all possible to find a location that will allow you to bring in your own outside catering and alcohol, do it," Sinn says. "It will save you thousands."

Source: Lacey Sinn, Development Director, Idaho Federation of Families for Children's Mental Health, Boise, ID. E-mail: lsinn@idahofederation.org

At a Glance —

Event Type:	Bachelor Auction
Gross:	$11,100
Costs:	$2,000
Net Income:	$9,100
Volunteers:	7
Planning:	120 hours beginning six months prior to event
Attendees:	157
Revenue Sources:	Ticket sales, live and silent auctions, cash donations
Unique Feature:	Hosted hors d'oeuvres, beer, wine and professional photographer who takes photos of attendees with bachelors

Content not available in this edition

Get Your Special Event Attendees in the Bidding Mood

When live auctions are part of your gala fundraiser, you have two major challenges: Finding desirable, big-ticket items from donors, and getting your audience in the right bidding mood.

Many variables impact patrons' feelings while the auction is in progress, such as:

✓ Did they enjoy their dinner and believe it was worth the ticket price?

✓ Is the room well-lit and comfortable?

✓ Are the registration and bidding processes simple to understand and unintimidating for newcomers?

✓ Are acoustics good enough so the auctioneer can be heard?

Consider these issues as you begin planning your special event:

- **'Tis it the season to be jolly?** Auctions during the end-of-year holiday season can be iffy for several reasons. People may be feeling tapped out financially and emotionally from gift shopping or uneasy about year-end financial reports. At the same time, people may feel especially generous at this heartwarming time of year. Take a look at your area's overall economy and determine if it has affected your supporters for the better. Spring might be a better time for a fundraiser when most people are feeling optimistic and upbeat.

- **Find a personable auctioneer or celebrity.** A local notable, or one of your most colorful staff or board members, may be a good choice. A team of two can be effective, too, especially if the guests enjoy the chemistry between them.

- **Keep it short and sweet.** By offering fewer, but higher-quality items, participants won't be as likely to be scanning the program to see how far down the list you are, and how many more items are left before they can exit gracefully.

- **Show the audience the goods.** A fur coat or diamond ring are very portable, and a young model can easily stroll through the tables during the bidding to show interested parties the merchandise, try it on themselves or touch it. Purebred puppies are another auction favorite that should be seen and enjoyed while the auction is taking place.

- **Set the mood for each item.** Have appropriate music or dance to introduce each attraction. A hula dancer for a Hawaiian vacation, a singing cowboy for a trip to the Grand Canyon or a chorus girl for a Las Vegas getaway make the auction seem more like an entertaining show.

- **Advertise the most desirable selections before the event.** When you mail the invitations, design an attractive insert to show guests some of the exciting possibilities: a limited edition work of art, a brand-new, fully loaded vehicle, an exotic piece of gemstone jewelry from a famous store or collectible autographed items can build anticipation and help guests plan which items most interest them — serious buyers will come prepared, and if they are outbid, they may console themselves with their second choice!

- **Ask popular contributors to act as spotters.** If a guest's friends are milling about keeping track of bids, they may bid more quickly when cajoled and encouraged by someone they like and know well. Good-natured competition, moderated by a friendly third party, can result in record high donations while a good time is being had by all.

- **Be sure guests can see all merchandise before the event.** Let them sit in cars, try on furs and jewelry, or play with exotic pets before bidding begins, as well as during the auction. Few buyers will offer significant amounts for merchandise they can't (at least partially) evaluate or see a practical use for in their lives.

The level of collective enthusiasm plays a key role in an auction's bidding process. These strategies will help to maximize the liveliness of your crowd and get them active in supporting your efforts through the auction.

Tip: The best-selling auction items are those with sentimental value. Amid the expected big-screen TVs and jewelry, locate some one-of-a-kind items or opportunities that have a connection to your organization — and to bidders' hearts.

Plan Ahead to Avoid Top 10 Auction Mistakes

Do you have a silent, live or online auction planned as part of your special event? Don't let all your auction preparation time, gift solicitation, organization and packaging go to waste because of simple, avoidable mistakes.

Charity auctioneer Lance Walker, who conducts some 100 fundraising auctions and workshops for charities throughout North America each year, cites the Top 10 mistakes made by event planners:

10. Not having all the auctions in the same room.

9. Not displaying items well and not using slides or video to spotlight items during the auction.

8. Having poor lighting. Brighter is better.

7. Using small bid numbers or not using bid numbers at all.

6. Closing the silent booths before dinner. Keeping them open holds people longer, increases profits and helps keep attendees entertained.

5. Starting the live auction too late or not on time. With 20 items or less, start later than usual.

4. Having too few energetic spotters to catch bids and keep the mood lively.

3. Beginning the live auction after the sit-down dinner is over. People are at their best while eating.

2. Relying on insufficient sound system. Use at least four large speakers on stands in each corner.

1. Not utilizing a dynamic professional fundraising auctioneer. Don't wait until the last minute to line up this key player.

"Many other mistakes can be and are made," Walker contends, "but auctions continue to be a great way to raise consistent revenue and promote good will among constituents."

Source: Lance Walker, Walker Auctions, Germantown, TN. E-mail: lance@walkerauctions.com

Gala Spotlight ...

Auction Gala Raises More Than $100,000 Annually

The Annual Auction Gala of The Covenant School is an 18-year tradition in Charlottesville, VA, that regularly raises $100,000-plus. Headmaster Emeritus and Director of Advancement Roland Sykes says there is no one formula for building a beloved community event, but does identify steps organizers can take to establish a successful auction gala:

- **Take responsibility for the success of bidding.** Live auction items cannot be allowed to sell for too low a price or donors' feelings will be hurt, says Sykes. Organizers must therefore be prepared to bid on floundering items, even if they don't want them. Sykes says he and his wife once bid up and eventually bought a week's stay at a condo in Puerto Vallarta simply because few other bids were being made.

- **Focus on entertainment.** Auctions focus on bidding and buying, but the real draw for most attendees is an evening of entertainment, says Sykes. "A good live auctioneer is worth his weight in gold, and a couple lively, outgoing spotters can engage the audience for hours of fun."

At a Glance —	
Event Type:	Auction Gala
Gross:	$104,000
Costs:	$14,000
Net Income:	$90,000
Volunteers:	50
Planning:	6 months
Attendees:	300
Revenue Sources:	Live and silent auctions, ticket sales, corporate sponsorships
Unique Feature:	With a school enrollment of around 500, the auction involves almost all student families

- **Establish strong committees and plenty of them.** The gala is almost entirely parent-run, says Sykes, noting that the event relies on six volunteer committees comprised of six to 10 members each. These committees handle everything from acquisitions and food to set up/take down, sponsorships and advertising.

- **Involve families of means.** The auction is a great way to get new families involved with the school, and Sykes makes a point of reaching out to those with significant means. "This year we identified six new families who could easily make major donations to the school, and had the chair of the auction invite the wives to help plan the auction. It's a powerful way to help people take ownership in the school."

- **Diversify funding streams.** Auction gala revenue comes from three relatively even streams, says Sykes. "A third comes from pre-selling sponsorships and advertising, a third comes from a silent auction of 300-plus items, and a third from a live auction of 20 to 25 items."

- **Sponsorship, sponsorship, sponsorship.** Of the three main revenue streams, sponsorship has the greatest potential for growth, says Sykes. This area, therefore, receives special attention, such as the school's 12 board members personally seeking and soliciting sponsorships.

Source: Ronald Sykes, Director of Advancement, The Covenant School, Charlottesville, VA. E-mail: rsykes@covenantschool.org

Boost Auction Inventory by Sharing List of Meal Possibilities

Planning a live or silent auction? Develop a list of meal ideas for people to choose from and donate as auction packages. Here are ideas to get you started:

- ❑ Tuscan dinner party
- ❑ Prohibition-era speakeasy
- ❑ Kentucky Derby affair
- ❑ Old-fashioned picnic
- ❑ Desserts to die for...
- ❑ Chocoholic's paradise
- ❑ Romantic, intimate dinner
- ❑ Mexican dinner party

- ❑ Tailgating theme
- ❑ Western-themed BBQ
- ❑ Breakfast at Tiffany's
- ❑ Retro '50s-style dinner
- ❑ Hawaiian luau
- ❑ Spanish dinner party with tapas
- ❑ Meal based on a movie
- ❑ Japanese-themed sushi party

Electronic Silent Auction Technology Boosts Event

For more than 20 years, the Dinner in the Stacks annual fundraiser at the Burton Barr Central Library (Phoenix, AZ) has been a staple of the area's social calendar, raising hundreds of thousands of dollars for literacy programs and other worthy causes.

Staged by The Phoenix Public Library Foundation (Phoenix, AZ), the event is the library's premier annual fundraiser. It features components such as a cocktail hour, silent auction and dinner.

The 2010 event drew 600 attendees, netted more than $200,000 and added a high-tech twist.

Foundation Director Geraldine Hills says the event's silent auction went to an electronic format in 2010. Foundation officials worked with IML Worldwide (www.imleventtechnology.com), which provided hand-held devices that guests used to bid on the silent auction items.

The use of the hand-held devices allowed the bidding to stay open longer and let guests post Twitter messages, egging each other on and driving up the bids. On average, Hills says, the electronic format has the potential to increase proceeds by 35 percent, though the silent auction at the 2010 event saw significantly less growth, reflecting challenges common to all Phoenix-based events.

During the program, guests were also given the chance to use their bidding devices to make pledges. Volunteers were in place to work with guests who needed help with the high-tech devices.

For the 2011 event, organizers planned to add an online component to allow people to bid on silent auction items remotely if they couldn't attend the fundraiser. Changes to the configuration of the event were also possible as well, Hills says, thanks to added flexibility from the electronic format of the silent auction.

"The Phoenix Public Library Foundation considered expanding the changes to the event for 2011, moving to more of a food station, multiple-activity event than a formal sit-down dinner," Hills says. "The electronic format will help us restructure the event and use more of the library for the event."

Source: Geraldine Hills, Director, The Phoenix Public Library Foundation, Phoenix, AZ. E-mail: Geraldine.Hills@phoenix.gov

Raffle Ticket Selling Methods

Here are ideas to get large numbers of raffle tickets sold:

1. Motivate sellers by offering a prize to the person/group who sells the most tickets.

2. Ask area businesses to have tickets available for sale. Use the same businesses every year so buyers know where to go.

3. Have tickets available for sale at the businesses that donated items (e.g., travel agencies, car dealerships, restaurants, hotels, electronic stores, etc.).

4. Keep a list of the previous year's buyers and give it to your sellers. You can create tickets where a stub with contact information is kept by your organization.

5. Ask your connected board members, staff and other volunteers to sell tickets.

6. For member-run organizations (e.g., a Rotary Club), use peer pressure to get members to sell or buy a certain amount of tickets. This usually works best with lower-priced tickets.

7. Offer a bulk-price deal on tickets: Buy 10, get one free.

8. Set up volunteer-run booths at county fairs and city festivals.

9. Offer at least one big-ticket item to drive interest and sales.

Handheld Devices Add Excitement, Profits to Event

Technological tools can boost bidding for your silent or live auction.

Natalie Leek-Nelson, CEO and president of Providence House (Cleveland, OH) says her organization had researched electronic bidding for its Deck the House Live & Silent Holiday Auction in the past, but nothing clicked until staff happened upon BidPal offered by BidPal Network (Indianapolis, IN).

By automating the silent auction using iPod Touch devices, Leek-Nelson says the organization actually boosted live auction proceeds by 14 percent.

"Guests loved the fact that they could bid on the live auction without losing a silent auction package," she says. "A good number said this was the first time they had participated in the live auction because in the past they were too focused on monitoring their silent auction bid slips throughout the room."

Leek-Nelson says each of the 700-plus guests had a bidding device linked to a system network constructed at the event site by BidPal staff. The devices let guests see photos and read descriptions of auction items, bid and manage maximum bids and outbids and receive a consolidated invoice (for live and silent auctions and general donations) at the evening's end, easing the checkout process for bidders, event staff and volunteers.

"We wanted to create a fun and exciting social atmosphere, while continuing to position Providence House as an innovator in fundraising events in the greater Cleveland community — and we did," says Leek-Nelson. "We have fielded calls from nearly 20 nonprofits throughout our region that heard about BidPal from our guests and want more information. The introduction of BidPal added excitement and kept people bidding. It was all in the palm of their hand!"

Providence House paid BidPal has a base booking fee (based on the estimated number of iPod Touch handheld devices the organization anticipates needing for the auction), a venue charge and travel expenses totaling approximately $8,000. She says they also paid BidPal a percentage of the proceeds based on the total dollars raised in the silent auction.

BidPal staff set up the system network onsite and provided Providence House staff with system training, an event support person, an on-site event support team and automated reports post-event.

Along with electronic bidding at the event and onsite support, BidPal officials also provided automated reporting functions that made it easier for staff to follow up on unclaimed and unpaid auction packages. Says Leek-Nelson, "From overall performance to item-by-item analysis, we could see everything from frequency of bids and outbids to bids exceeding retail values and more. They really helped us zero in on the most successful items for next year."

Leek-Nelson says that a sponsor underwrote the cost of the BidPal system, and is considering doing so again for this year's event.

Source: Natalie Leek-Nelson, CEO and President, Providence House, Cleveland, OH. E-mail: natalie@provhouse.org.

Four Tips for Taking on Electronic Bidding

CEO and President Natalie Leek-Nelson, Providence House (Cleveland, OH), says her organization researched several electronic bidding systems and companies before moving forward with BidPal (Indianapolis, IN). She shares some of the lessons learned in the process to benefit other organizations seeking to expand into electronic bidding:

1. Ask plenty of questions before signing an agreement.

2. Consider your specific event. The Providence House's event is an open floor, roaming event without a formal sit-down program, so handheld devices worked well. If your event requires guests to focus without distraction, these might not be for you, because everyone is clicking and scrolling all night long.

3. Keep the learning curve in mind. When implementing new technology into an event, prepare to work ahead to educate the committee, staff and volunteers on using the technology and offering guests support during the event.

4. Train some reliable volunteers to help at your event. Leek-Nelson says some guests needed additional assistance with the new technology, which they provided through volunteer support from a local high school's technology club.

How to Plan Profitable, WOW-Factor Galas

CREATING A CROWD-PLEASING EXPERIENCE

Looking for ways to make your gala fun and exciting for your guests? Look no further. Check out these examples of crowd-pleasing ideas.

Surprise Elements Keep Audiences Intrigued, Delighted

People look forward to your organization's parties not only because they support a worthy cause, but also because they are festive and entertaining. You want to keep attendees coming back by offering fresh activities and features. Here are some tips for serving up an element of surprise:

✓ **Transform an ordinary facility.** Incorporating elements like dramatic tension structures and lighting can turn a gymnasium into a movie set.

✓ **Invite an unexpected VIP guest.** Does a nationally known figure or entertainer have ties to your community? Whom do your contacts know who might enjoy coming to your event if they won't be dogged by the media?

✓ **Feature artistic food.** Delight guests with ornate edible centerpieces, fruit bouquets, dessert towers and even ice sculptures.

✓ **Give generous prizes to random guests.** It's popular to offer floral centerpieces to the person at the table whose birthday is closest to the event's date to take home. Stick a $100 gift card from a local retailer on the bottom.

✓ **Present an unexpected major award.** You'll want to ensure in advance that the recipient will attend, then honor them with a musical and video tribute.

✓ **Hire surprise entertainment.** Your audience expects your local jazz quintet, but imagine their delight if a world-famous band shows up on stage after the opening act.

✓ **Light up the sky.** Announce that there will be a special event at the end of the evening. Then begin a spectacular fireworks display with a theme that has special meaning for your organization.

✓ **Save a pivotal announcement for the occasion.** You have reached a fundraising goal that allows you to break ground on a new facility. You have made an important alliance that will allow you to reach national or worldwide audiences. Share the good news with your most loyal supporters in a festive environment first.

Tip: Which is more dramatic: A summer beach in January, or a winter wonderland in July? Both can make for memorable themes for a special event.

Give guests a welcome break from the current season with a few hours immersed in the best its opposite has to offer.

Chance for Treasure Holds Guests' Interest

At the Culinary Cabaret for Holland Hospital Foundation (Holland, MI), having the right ticket could mean winning a diamond necklace, which is just one highlight of the well-attended event, says Executive Director Sue Ann Culp.

For a chance at the treasure, persons purchase a gourmet chocolate bar for $25 from sellers who mingle through the crowd. Inside 10 of the treats are gold-colored tickets that entitle the bearer a chance to choose a key. One of the 10 keys opens a display case holding the diamond necklace. A local company underwrites the cost of the necklace, which a local jeweler creates at cost.

Culinary Cabaret guests are also invited to vote for the most creative display and the tastiest cuisine out of the 12 to 14 higher-end local restaurants offering appetizer-size cuisine representing their various specialties. Guests who vote are entered into a drawing to receive a $100 gift certificate to the participating restaurant of their choice.

The winning restaurants and chefs receive medallions, plaques, and feature placement in a newspaper ad.

Source: Sue Ann Culp, Executive Director, Holland Hospital Foundation, Holland, MI.
E-mail: saculp@hollandhospital.org

Gala Spotlight ...

Brewers Bazaar Draws Attention, Crowds

Officials at the Stillwater Sunrise Rotary Club (Stillwater, MN) were looking for a fundraiser that went beyond the typical silent auction/dinner/gala.

The event they eventually founded — the Brewers Bazaar — does that and more. The annual beer-tasting festival, now entering its fifth year, regularly draws 500-plus attendees and raises over $12,000.

The event was an easy sell when officials first approached local brewers in 2007, says Paula Williams, event organizer.

"We offered a $150 stipend for the first time this year, but most of the brewers donated it back to the club. They are there strictly to promote their beers," she says, noting that the festival's one-on-one interaction with potential customers is more than enough incentive for most brewers.

Williams says the event attracts 12 to 15 brewers a year, most of whom bring 2 to 5 types of beer. For a $30 entrance ticket, attendees can try as many samples as they like while enjoying on-site entertainment like live music and beer-making demonstrations.

Staged on a paddle boat on the St. Croix River, the event is also held in conjunction with a local art fair, allowing fairgoers to visit the bazaar and viceversa.

The event typically takes about four months to plan and relies on around 40 day-of volunteers, says Williams. Ticket sales and corporate sponsorship provide the majority of the revenue, though funds are boosted by a raffle and revenue-sharing agreements with a few food vendors and service providers.

Williams says Stillwater is fortunate to have a long tradition of locally produced craft brewing, but she hastens to add that other areas need not avoid beer-tasting events. "From what our brewers have told us, they will travel quite extensively throughout a region to attend a viable tasting event."

She adds that individuals who attend beer festivals often follow favorite brewers with great loyalty, both from festival to festival and year to year. "If you can attract some quality brewers, you can count on a certain number of yearly attendees, which is always helpful."

Source: Paula Williams, Stillwater Sunrise Rotary Club, Stillwater, MN.
E-mail: Pwilliams@lakeareabank.com.

At a Glance —

Event Type:	Beer Tasting
Gross:	$20,000
Costs:	$8,000
Net Income:	$12,000
Volunteers:	40
Planning:	4 months
Attendees:	450 to 600
Revenue Sources:	Ticket sales, raffle concessions, corporate sponsorships and profit sharing with selected vendors.
Unique Feature:	Held aboard a working river paddle boat.

Manage Alcohol-related Risks

Though alcohol can boost revenue for an event, it also presents unique challenges. Paula Williams, organizer of the Stillwater Sunrise Rotary Club's (Stillwater, MN) Brewers Bazaar, shares some of the precautions her organization took to minimize alcohol-related risks:

- **Small glasses.** "One thing we learned through experience is that if you get 16-ounce glasses, the brewers will fill them up, and people will be doing more than tasting," says Williams. "So now we make sure we order glasses that are seven ounces or smaller."

- **Small pours.** "We always instruct the brewers to pour only an inch or less," says Williams. She adds that while brewers might not all follow these directions, the organization at least set an acceptable standard.

- **Follow local ordinances.** Event organizers are careful to follow all local ordinances, such as having an off-duty police officer present at all times during the event, says Williams.

- **No sales.** Williams says it's important to not mix selling and sampling. "The riverboat we were on had its own liquor license, governing the sale of alcohol there, so we made sure nothing was sold during the event."

Flash Mob Provides Crowd Control, Creates Excitement at Gala

The problem was one many gala-type events face: transitioning 900 guests from cocktail hour to dinner quickly enough to stay on schedule. The solution devised by officials at Tipping Point, a San Francisco-based nonprofit dedicated to fighting poverty and known for creativity in its fundraising events, was as unique as it was attention grabbing: staging a flash mob.

"Basically, a flash mob is when one person in a crowd breaks out into a choreographed dance routine, and as the background music builds, more and more dancers join in," says Jaime Law, senior associate for communication and events.

In the case of the Tipping Point event, the mob ultimately included 120 volunteers, board members and staff members, all of whom pretended to be regular guests until their cue to join in. The overall effect, says Law, was a "surprise moment" that was highly entertaining and memorable.

Law says a local high school dance teacher choreographed the three-minute performance. It relied on a core group of about 20 professional and amateur dancers who learned the entire routine and helped teach the remaining participants over the course of four collective practices, including a dress rehearsal the night before.

How did the performance help the group transition from cocktails to dinner? When the song ended, doors to the meal area opened, the dancers streamed in and guests followed. (Other volunteers in the cocktail area urged stragglers along.) Seating was accomplished in about 10 minutes — far less time than in past years.

But Law says the tone set for the evening was just as important. "People were really excited about what was ahead after that," she says. "The flash mob was a really fresh and fun way to engage stakeholders in a unique and memorable experience."

The 2011 gala raised a record $6.5 million — $500,000 more than the previous year — and the YouTube video of the performance (http://www.youtube.com/watch?v=qU1MC4voURY) has received over 12,000 views.

Source: Jaime Law, Senior Associate for Communication and Events, Tipping Point, San Francisco, CA. E-mail: Jlaw@tippingpoint.org

Practice at Home Crucial To Staging a Flash Mob

Are you interested in flash mob performance, but worried it might require more practice time than your organization can spare? Get your dance company in top shape by providing rookies with a way to improve on their own.

Officials at Tipping Point did this by posting a tutorial video on YouTube to facilitate practice at home. This allowed participants to develop the confidence needed to just enjoy the performance, says Jaime Law, senior associate for communication and events.

"Having a good time is central to the whole idea," she says. "When people are really having a good time, they give off a kind of energy that is very contagious and just fills the whole room."

Involve More Guests With Entertaining Activities

Raising funds for and increasing awareness of your mission may be the purpose of your event, but many who attend will see it as an opportunity to have fun and socialize.

Here are some tips you can use to help increase audience involvement and entertainment.

- **Create a central attraction in the middle of the room**, like a large cupcake display or dance floor so everyone feels involved regardless of seating assignment.

- **Adapt an audience participation game** like "Let's Make a Deal" or "The Price Is Right" to your program where any guest has a chance to be on stage or win a prize.

- **Offer a scavenger hunt.** Compile a list of common items (shoelace, nail clipper, pocketknife, flashlight) that guests might not normally carry to a party. Ask those who have the item to share why they brought them.

- **Try Name That Tune!** Everyone has a party horn. Play snippets of music to see who can identify it first by blowing their horn. Let the top players compete for a grand prize.

- **Feature some popular casino games.** Have a few that require skill, like blackjack, and others like roulette or dice that anyone can play.

- **Hire a cartoonist.** A quick sketch artist can float between tables drawing guests, and then make a display at the end of the evening for all to view.

- **Suggest a table switch.** Put five or six different colors of decoration on individual desserts. Ask each person to have the last course with someone else who has a green flower, an orange star or a purple crown.

How to Plan Profitable, WOW-Factor Galas

How to Get a Celebrity to Emcee Your Event

Few factors attract a greater turnout to special events than having a celebrity as your master or mistress of ceremonies. But for a locally based nonprofit with limited resources, landing a famous name as emcee may seem out of reach.

Sharing tips to help boost your chances of landing a big name — and all the attention that goes with it — are special event experts Darlene Tenes, founder and CEO of Marketing Maniacs (San Jose, CA), a public relations and marketing firm that has worked with numerous nonprofits, and Bonnie Vent, owner of Genesis Creations Entertainment (San Diego, CA), a celebrity booking service.

First, Vent says, know that you may need to pay an appearance fee. "Some small nonprofits start off with unrealistic expectations. They assume all celebrities are very wealthy and will come to their event on their own dime. Unless the celebrity is a close, personal friend, they will expect some sort of payment for their services and want their travel expenses to be covered."

So how much should you expect to pay?

Celebrity appearance fees start at $5,000 to $10,000, and some will discount for nonprofits, Vent says. There are ways to book a celebrity for considerably less, however, as well as ways to ensure the most bang for your buck.

For example, Vent recommends booking a celebrity two to three months in advance to give time to properly promote his/her name to increase ticket sales.

You should also strive to "maximize the celebrity's time," Vent says. "People will say they only need the celebrity for two hours and want to pay an hourly rate. Keep in mind that they will be flying in the day before the event and out the day after. Take advantage of the time they are there. No matter what, it is three days of the celebrity's time."

Think Local for Celebrity Emcee

Local newscasters are always a good bet when it comes to snagging a well-known name at no cost to emcee your event. Most will be happy to help. Moreover, since they are local, they will have little or no travel expense, and may even provide some on-air coverage for your event.

If you have a specific newscaster in mind, send him/her an impassioned letter explaining in detail why you'd be thrilled if he/she would consider serving as your emcee. Be specific. Will his/her personality add a fun, memorable component to the evening? Or perhaps he/she recently reported on an event that has ties to your cause.

If you're not as particular about which local celebrity you land, call up the station and ask to speak to whomever handles community outreach. Again, explain with enthusiasm why your special event would benefit from a member of their on-camera news staff.

Begin your search at least three months in advance, just as you would with a celebrity of national scope. Just because a local newscaster doesn't need to make travel arrangements or isn't as in demand doesn't mean his/her time should not be equally respected.

Luck and timing play roles in landing a celebrity for little or free, so be prepared when an opportunity comes along. Keep a wish list of most-wanted names by finding celebrities with personal tie-ins to your cause or another personal connection to your organization, says Darlene Tenes, founder and CEO of Marketing Maniacs (San Jose, CA), a public relations and marketing firm that has worked with numerous nonprofits.

On your favorite online search engine, enter the word "celebrity" plus a phrase that describes your cause. Look through issues of People and Parade magazines, which often write about celebrity-affiliated causes. Find out if anybody famous attended a local school, has family in the area or lives nearby, says Tenes. Ask everyone on your board, your employees and volunteers — if they have a personal connection to someone well-known.

Once you have your list, crosscheck it with celebrity events in your region such as concerts, film shoots or promotional tours. "Check ticketing and arena websites to see who's going to be in town at the same time as your event — this saves on travel costs," Tenes says. "Or you can split costs with another promoter."

When you have a specific celebrity in mind, do an online search for the celebrity's name plus the words "publicist" or "media contact," says Tenes. Use the information you find, she says, to "contact their management to request a special appearance. Keep the e-mail short with the facts: date, time, location and what is expected of them."

Your goal, says Tenes, should be to make it "really convenient for them to attend" while also "having some benefit for them." If you can provide both at once, you have a shot at a famous name for free.

Sources: Darlene Tenes, Founder and CEO, Marketing Maniacs, San Jose, CA. E-mail: darlene@maniacidea.com.
Bonnie Vent, Owner, Genesis Creations Entertainment, Chula Vista, CA. E-mail: bvent@genesiscreations.biz.

Gala Spotlight ...

March Martini Madness Mixes Sophistication, 1960s Style

The style! The sophistication! The cocktails!

Why did the Yakima Valley Museum (Yakima, WA) turn to AMC's hit show "Mad Men" for a new fundraising theme?

Demographics, says David Lynx, associate director.

"We had a solid base of patrons, but we were looking for ways to reach out to that 25-to-55 age range," Lynx says. "The mad atmosphere of March Martini Madness created a cool, hip kind of ambiance that really spoke to the crowd we were targeting."

The nighttime event in the museum's neon garden atrium oozed retro 1960s elegance at every turn with gourmet hors d'oeuvres, cigarette girls selling raffle tickets and rat pack music sung by a wandering crooner.

Also central to the event's appeal were three individually themed martini bars. Staffed by bartenders dressed like Marilyn Monroe, Frank Sinatra and James Bond, each sold two or three specialized martinis. A juice bar provided stylish concoctions to those avoiding alcohol.

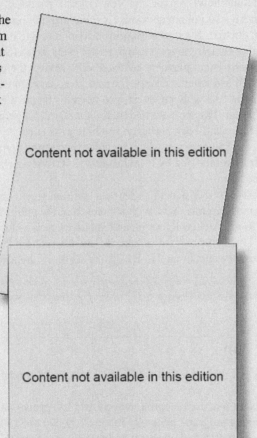

Content not available in this edition

Content not available in this edition

The sold-out event raised more than $12,000. More importantly, organizers say, it drew a new and younger group of supporters. Lynx estimates that half of the 200 guests were first-time supporters, and he expects that number to grow for future events through strong word-of-mouth promotion.

"People were telling everyone how great a time they had, and there is a lot of excitement for the second Martini Madness," he says, adding that museum staff are already pursuing more robust corporate underwriting to help translate community interest into usable revenue.

Source: David Lynx, Associate Director, Yakima Valley Museum, Yakima, WA. E-mail: David@yakimavalleymuseum.org

Eight Tips to Set Event Mood

Setting a particular mood when planning an event is an important way to convey its reason or purpose, says Nicole Bennett, owner of the event and meeting services company, Perry Consulting LLC (Phoenix, AZ). She shares tips to carry out the spirit of your event:

1. The mood begins with the invitations, so make sure they capture the proper feel and set guests' expectations for your event.

2. Decor plays an important role, with lighting taking center stage. If you want the most bang for your buck, allocate some money to lighting. Work with an audiovisual company whose team can suggest options that will help create the impact you seek. Can't afford specialty lighting? Make the most of what you have available.

3. If you have the budget for it, hire roaming entertainment to create a lively and memorable atmosphere.

4. To create mood without a lot of money, start with what you have on hand. Does your office have plants or other decor you can move to the event venue? Watch seasonal sales for items to use for future events. Using real flowers? Ask your florist for seasonal flowers rather than requesting a special order, and if you can rent vases.

5. Favors can do double duty as event decor and keepsakes for guests to take home as a reminder of your event.

6. Entertainment is another way to infuse your event with a theme/mood.

7. Don't forget about external influences that could make or break the mood. Provide accurate directions and ample parking so guests arrive in a mood that will allow them to immerse themselves joyfully in the environment.

8. Finally, whatever mood you decide to create, make sure warmth and hospitality are the foundation — how your guests are treated will ultimately be what they remember most!

Source: Nicole V. Bennett, Owner, Perry Consulting, LLC, Laveen, AZ.

Offer Guests Reasons to Don Costumes

The Feeding Friend-zy fundraiser at The Children's Museum of Wilmington (Wilmington, NC) brings in as much as $80,000, but what makes this annual event unique is that it has people pulling out costumes in the middle of February to match that year's theme.

For 2011, the theme focused on Hollywood.

"We had a red carpet, it was Oscar week, and having everyone dress up like Hollywood added to the fun of the event," says Rick Lawson, executive director of the museum. Many of the people in attendance even got together as a group and dressed as characters from a certain movie. "We had 'Toy Story', 'City Slickers' and 'Raiders of the Lost Ark'," says Lawson.

Past years' themes include: cowboys; "Grease" the movie; olympics sports/countries; pirates; and Superbowl champs, the New Orleans' Saints.

Lawson says 10 volunteers work for months planning the event, serving on four key committees: auction; food; event staging/decoration; and marketing. Each committee meets monthly and eventually twice a month as the event gets closer, says Lawson.

Each March, event planners get together to review the prior month's event, discussing what went well and what to change for next year, says Katie Daniel, the museum's director of development. "As with any event, you need to change the format and feel of the event based on the year. This year we had more of a glam Hollywood feel, next year we may change to a more laid-back barbeque and bluegrass event."

Tickets are $50 a person which includes dinner and dancing. There is also a silent auction with items donated by local businesses. Lawson says yoga lessons were a hot item in this year's auction.

The event draws 250 to 350 attendees and runs from 7 p.m. to midnight. Invitations are e-mailed to museum members, with anyone from the public invited to attend.

"We also give tickets to our exhibit sponsors such as local grocery stores and businesses. This helps to create a buzz around town about the museum," says Lawson.

Attendees are encouraged to RSVP, but walk-ins are also welcome that night.

Sources: Katie Daniel, Director of Development; Rick Lawson, Executive Director; The Children's Museum of Wilmington, Wilmington, NC. E-mail: kdaniel@playwilmington.org or rlawson@playwilmington.org

Game Theme Adds Gala Fun

It seems as if Mr. Moneybag's luck has rubbed off on the Holland Hospital Foundation (Holland, MI) and its Monopoly-themed gala event.

The annual event, which started as a donor recognition event and has grown into a fundraising event to support the foundation's school nursing program, generally raises $100,000 to $130,000.

Organizers retooled the event in 2010 to add more fun and make it less formal, says Executive Director Sue Ann Culp. They chose a theme based on Hasbro's iconic Monopoly board game, replacing a sit-down dinner with food-tasting stations representing Monopoly board properties and a beverage bar named for the game's Water Works utilities property.

Black top hats filled with flowers and Monopoly pieces decorated the tables, and the emcee dressed as Mr. Moneybags, the top-hat wearing, cane-carrying, mustache-sporting Monopoly mascot. Culp says the casual atmosphere allowed guests to network as they visited food stations, then viewed a short video about school nursing and heard brief remarks from the event's co-chairs, followed by a dance featuring a live dance band.

Because of an existing endowment, 100 percent of partnership money, individual donations and grants goes directly to providing health care services to uninsured/underinsured members of the community. Says Culp, "This is a critical marketing piece that makes a gift to our organization different from others in the area. Our donors know that if they give us $1, the full $1 goes to help people in need."

The 2010 event raised $126,000 and drew 230 guests. Sources of revenue included partnerships with local businesses and ticket sales.

Source: Sue Ann Culp, Executive Director, Holland Hospital Foundation, Holland, MI. E-mail: saculp@hollandhospital.org

Gala Spotlight ...

Dance-themed Gala Raises Funds, Awareness

A unique name and a memorable theme combine in an annual gala that raises money for Children & Families of Iowa (CFI) of Des Moines, IA.

The 2009 Tango raised more than $177,000 and drew 467 attendees — with each $86 ticket sold representing one night of shelter and services for one victim.

"The name for the event used to be Tango on the Terrace because we had it outside on a terrace overlooking the city," says Susan Joynt, event manager. "However, we ran into bad weather, either rain or very high temperatures, year after year that caused us to move the event inside, so we shortened the name to Tango. We use different dance names for levels of giving, Tango being the highest level of corporate support, then Salsa, Rumba and Mamba."

With the additional funds raised through sponsorships and auctions, event organizers estimated the proceeds from the 2009 event would provide 2,000 nights of shelter and services at CFI's domestic violence programs or a month of care for a capacity shelter.

The nonprofit provides shelter, advocacy and outreach for more than 7,000 victims of domestic violence every year. CFI reports that in the past year, the program has seen a 38 percent increase in crisis calls and 13 percent increase in need for safe shelter.

In the past five years, the organization has served more than 44,000 persons.

Follow these tips offered by event planners at CFI to produce a quality gala event:

- ❑ Establish a good reputation. CFI is an established nonprofit with a good reputation in the community. The Tango gala event is also well-established in its seventh year.

- ❑ Establish the cause for guests. The money raised is designated to support CFI's domestic violence services.

- ❑ Tie the event into the cause. Tango ticket pricing directly reflects the cost of one night of shelter and services for a person fleeing a violent situation.

Source: Susan Joynt, Events Manager, Children & Families of Iowa, Des Moines, IA. E-mail: susanj@CFIOWA.org.

At a Glance —	
Event Type:	Gala event
Gross:	$177,000-plus
Costs:	$31,000
Net Income:	$147,000
Volunteers:	20-25 (to solicit corporate donations and silent auction donations; help with catering, invitations and set up)
Planning:	6-8 months
Attendees:	467
Revenue Sources:	Ticket sales, corporate sponsorship, live and silent auctions
Unique Feature:	Ticket price based on cost to provide one night of service in domestic violence shelter

Content not available in this edition

Disco-themed Parties Offer Built-in Fun

If you're in your 50s or older, you remember and probably participated in the 1970s disco craze. Bring back some of the energy and excitement of those days at your next fundraiser with a themed event that includes some of these activities:

- Wear a vintage disco dress or suit.

- Hold a dance contest with a special category for highest platform shoes.

- Dress as your favorite disco-era character — one of the Village People, Donna Summer or John Travolta are just a few suggestions.

- Award prizes for the best attire in couples, individual and celebrity look-a-like categories.

- Rent a lighted disco dance floor and the biggest mirrored disco ball you can find.

- Decorate with movie posters of popular films of the era like "Saturday Night Fever," "Rocky" and "Can't Stop the Music," just to name a few.

- Make your party drinks retro festive, including Mai Tais, piña coladas, whisky sours or mocktails that mimic the real thing.

- Enjoy popular disco club food with a buffet including cheese sticks, meatballs, cocktail sausages, egg rolls or chicken wings.

- Have a plentiful supply of fun party favors including glow-in-the-dark jewelry or disco ball key chains.

- Display hot vintage cars popular in the 1970s at your entrance, and have a red velvet rope to create a Studio 54 atmosphere.

- Hire professional dancers who can provide both entertainment and refresher courses in disco dancing.

- Include youngsters with a Disco Kids area where they can dance and play. Many of them will already know lots of the iconic songs and will enjoy dressing up.

- Party music is the easy part. Decide whether to hire a professional disc jockey or bring your own collection of CDs to play.

- Ask local singers or bands to come and create their own versions of Gloria Gaynor, the Bee Gees or Earth, Wind and Fire.

Tip: Nothing elicits "oohs and aahs" like a grand surprise. Think of it: A 50-piece symphony appears. A celebrity walks on stage. A major donor presents a check not only giant in size, but in amount. Brainstorm for ideas to punctuate your event with a grand gesture in an unexpected way.

After-party Event Engages Guests Longer

Offering guests the promise of an after-party is a creative way to keep them from leaving your event early and to make the fun last.

Organizers say an after-party is one of the highlights of the annual Woman Volunteer of the Year Luncheon and Fashion Show for the Junior League of Boca Raton (JLBR), Boca Raton, FL. This event — in its 23rd year — pulls in nearly 800 guests each October and keeps them socializing with the promise of an after-party.

The 2010 after-party included shopping for clothing, handbags, jewelry, cosmetics and accessories presented during a fashion show sponsored by Saks Fifth Avenue and Dior. A percentage of purchases made at the event supported the organization.

The event at the Boca Raton Resort & Club begins with a 10:30 a.m. reception followed by the luncheon. The after-party begins at 1:45 p.m. and continues to 4 p.m.

"The after-party is always a great opportunity for us to celebrate all of the nominees and the winner of the Woman Volunteer of the Year Award," says Samantha Vassallo, JLBR president.

Source: Melissa Montes, Public Relations and Marketing Chair, Junior League of Boca Raton, Boca Raton, FL. E-mail: mmontes814@gmail.com.

Create a Tropical Paradise

A tropical-themed event lends itself to colors, textures, shapes and scents that naturally create an inviting atmosphere for your guests. Here are some ways to lend some island flavor to your party:

- ❑ **Buy or borrow potted plants from a nursery or garden store.** Rhododendron or azalea bushes, hibiscus or palm trees work well in most temperate climates, indoors or out. After using them for your party, plant them on your facility grounds. Use pricier plants, like orchids, as centerpiece accents.

- ❑ **Use water features for scent and sound.** Attractive glass containers with brightly colored water and floating candles make affordable and beautiful centerpieces while providing soft light and fragrance. Use portable indoor-outdoor lighted water fountains in strategic locations.

- ❑ **Bring in brilliantly colored birds.** Local pet stores or supporters may be willing to allow their friendly parrots, toucans or other exotic winged pets to attend your event. They provide entertainment, real sound effects and natural color. Help make arrangements for safe transportation, and even help the pet store make a sale if a parrot and a guest form a bond.

- ❑ **Make or buy tropical light strings.** You may already have strings of tiny white lights in your event supplies closet. Add parts of deconstructed silk flowers to each bulb. Online party supply vendors also offer dozens of lantern and flower string selections for affordable prices. While flaming tiki torches may break fire regulations, a variety of solar- and battery-operated versions are available.

- ❑ **Add lighting and backdrops.** A blank screen and projected lighting can create a tropical sunset in any setting. A simple spotlight placed behind an arrangement of palms and ferns works in nearly any dull corner.

- ❑ **Choose appropriate fabric and materials.** Bamboo poles and cloth in a tropical pattern can go a long way in creating a tropical paradise. Floral patterns can range from sophisticated white palm leaves on green to funky flip-flops and sunglasses, depending on whether your crowd is all adults, or if children and families are the main audience.

Banners, Graphics Enhance Fundraising Theme

Attractive event banners not only announce this is the place, but can be focal points in your theme and decorations. The trick is to make sure they complement — rather than conflict with — the overall scheme.

- ✓ **Customize and personalize your banner.** Visit your local sign shop or fast-sign franchise to explore size, material, color and display options. Modern print technology makes it easier than ever to determine exactly what you want with prompt turnaround time and agreeable prices.

- ✓ **Design your own banner online.** Dozens of web resources have templates to create nearly any type and size banner using interactive tools, or to upload a complete image you or your graphic artist have designed. Your banner can coordinate seamlessly with your invitations and posters.

- ✓ **Check out banner materials for flexible options.** Imagine the visual impact of a bold banner stretched across the finish line of your race and the winner breaking through it as cameras roll and spectators cheer. Breakaway banners made of Velcro can be used more than once.

- ✓ **Make a light-box banner.** Fabric-faced LED light boxes allow you to use a standard flat surface or innovative three-dimensional shapes like cubes or panoramas, and to show your image from edge to edge.

- ✓ **Try floor or sidewalk graphics.** People expect to look up to see a banner, but custom sidewalk graphics can be creative stepping stones to lead guests to the party. Besides being colorful and attractive, they can be made in a wide range of sizes, used indoors or outdoors and provide a non-slip surface.

How to Plan Profitable, WOW-Factor Galas

POST-EVENT & EVALUATION PROCEDURES

Although you will no doubt be ready to call it a day once your gala is over, the evaluation procedures you take immediately following the event will make your next gala even better. Likewise, there are a number of important post-event actions you should take following your gala.

Plan for a Post-event Meeting

When creating your special event timeline, pencil in a post-event meeting.

Evaluating your event at a post-event gathering is an excellent way to improve your event next year. Follow these tips for your post-event wrap-up:

❑ Schedule the post-event meeting within two weeks of the event so it is fresh in the minds of the committee and/or organizers.

❑ The post-event meeting is a great time to offer kudos to volunteers and committee members. Share words of thanks and present tokens of appreciation at this time.

❑ Facilitate constructive criticism to improve future events. Ask post-event meeting attendees to complete a survey about the event to obtain suggestions to improve the event next year. Discuss the event and generate ideas from attendees with a free-flowing exchange of ideas, but avoid allowing it to turn into a gripe session. As the facilitator of the meeting, share your thoughts and ideas by starting with positives and ending with positives, then pass out the survey for attendees to complete.

❑ Follow up. After you collect the surveys, enjoy a time of community with attendees with a light luncheon as another way to express your gratitude for their service. Once the meeting is complete, review surveys and follow up with anyone who shared significant concerns about the event or offered particularly useful tips for next year.

❑ Record your findings and put new approaches into play for the next planning session. Once an event wraps, it's easy to walk away and forget it until next year. Instead, create a binder filled with the completed surveys, along with action points you develop following the post-event evaluation session to help you put your best foot forward next year.

Learn From Other Organizations' Events

Want to learn how various types of special events work and discover new features that you might want to add to an existing event? Make it your job to attend others' events.

Why not approach other noncompetitive nonprofits in your community or area and come up with a reciprocity agreement: If you can attend their special events for free, they can attend yours.

Having such an agreement in place will allow you to discover more about how a particular event works, and determine if such an event will work for your organization as well. And in those instances in which you have the same event, you can discover special features that you may want to incorporate into your event.

"But why would I want to share our events with other nonprofits' event planners? Why would I want them to see how we structure a particular event?"

First, there's nothing to prevent others from paying the price of ticket to attend, so you really have nothing to hide. Second, if you have confidence in your ability to pull off successful, highly attended events, then what do you have to lose?

If you're hesitant, try a reciprocity agreement with a couple of other nonprofits to test your comfort level. Then expand your pool of partners over time.

Tip: *Soon after your special event, send all attendees a personalized note thanking them for helping those served by your organization.*

Include Comprehensive Evaluation in Event Planning Procedures

Of all event planning steps, how important is the evaluation?

Very important, says Charles Hammersley, a professor who teaches within the Department of Geography, Planning and Recreation at Northern Arizona University (Flagstaff, AZ) and teaches a course for the university's Parks and Recreation Management Program on special events planning and evaluation.

"If you don't evaluate your events through your staff and also through your participants then you really have no objective measurement for success of the event," says Hammersley.

An evaluation form, he says, is an important method for evaluating your event and determining success. "It's very important to be able to standardize your evaluations so that you can track the events over time," he says. "If you do not standardize it with a form then whatever data you collect this time will not be the same data you collect next time, therefore you can't make any comparisons of your events. Standardization of your special event (through a) form allows for a comparison over time, which is very important in analyzing special event programs."

Determining Your Questions

Hammersley says the questions on the form should be unique to the event and to your community. "You have to first define what success is and how you define success is going to determine what type of information you want to collect," he says. "Of course, there is also standard information that we all want, such as the socio-demographic information which can include the numbers of people in attendance, the geographic location of individuals, residents, or visitors or businesses, as well as ages, party sizes and whether individuals are attending as an individual, group, or as a family. But after that, then it has to be specialized to the event and to the community."

Who Fills Out the Form: How to Keep it Consistent

Hammersley said that usually the event coordinator, event director or a specific person on your event staff should fill out the form. "That also provides consistency in how event forms are completed and how the events are scored," he says. "If you have the same person doing those forms then that allows for consistency of information."

Why Training is The Ticket to Motivation

To motivate people to complete forms, put it in their job requirement, Hammersley says. "You live and die for your special events by how well your staff is trained; probably the most important thing you can do for your event is train your staff and part of your staff training is emphasizing the importance of the evaluation process. If your staff buys into this and understands how important it is to evaluate, then it won't be problematic in getting your staff to complete those evaluations with a lot of forethought in how this will be used."

Why the Process Doesn't End With Filing Away the Form

After completing the form, use it, Hammersley says. "The information is worthless unless you use it for comparisons to prior events or to create a standardized data set for all of your events and so what you have to do is put it into a data set so you can pull that data up and you can compare it to other data you collected. Just storing it in a file and pulling it out next year is really not part of the evaluation process."

Hammersley says evaluation forms help improve Northern Arizona University's Verde River Canoe Challenge, an annual canoe race: "We do a lot of evaluations on that and we look at how far away people are coming to the event, how long they are staying, what type of boat they are using and then we compare that against a 10-year track record. That is a decade of evaluations and information that we can look at as we do our planning for the following year. This allows us to plan for the growth of the event and it allows us to plan for the outcomes and the participant satisfaction for that event as well. The most important part of using the form is being able to compare the information over time and using that to enhance your special event."

Source: Dr. Charles Hammersley, Northern Arizona University, Flagstaff, AZ.
E-mail: charles.hammersley@nau.edu

Content not available in this edition

Use Assessment Form to Measure Your Event's Success

Even if raising money is the primary goal of your special event, be sure to consider other factors when measuring its success. For instance, measure the event on whether it helps your organization achieve:

✓ **Community awareness.** Did the community learn more about your mission and programs from positive media coverage of the activity?

✓ **Participant awareness.** Was it clear that participants learned more about your organization and gained a deeper appreciation?

✓ **Event compatibility.** Was the nature of your event compatible with the audience you hoped to attract?

✓ **Chairperson/committee satisfaction.** Was your event chairperson and his/her committee upbeat about the outcome and attendance?

✓ **Overall volunteer satisfaction.** Did volunteers enjoy planning and executing the event as much as guests enjoyed attending?

✓ **Ease of planning.** Did the organizational system provide for a smooth planning process, start to finish?

✓ **Appropriate volunteer matching.** Were the talents and abilities of all volunteer participants used to the fullest, providing you increased insight for making future assignments that are rewarding?

✓ **New volunteer opportunities.** Did the event help attract new volunteers who see a place for their skills?

✓ **Business partnerships.** Did the business community gain insight into the potential benefits of their association with your organization?

Honestly assessing your event's success can only enhance its future. Volunteers will find it more rewarding and enjoyable. The event's objectives will be more fully realized. And your time in planning and executing the event will be used more productively.

Key Evaluation Questions

In evaluating your special events, large and small, come up with answers to the following key questions:

- Did it accomplish the goal (i.e., dollars raised or friends made or retained)?

- Was the mailing list broad enough? How could it be expanded next time?

- Were the costs low enough to make at least a 100 percent profit (e.g. cost per person was $25 and you made $12.50 on each ticket)?

- Did the event's publicity benefit the organization? Who did you contact? What coverage did you receive?

- Is interest/attendance in the event increasing or decreasing? If attendance is decreasing, why? How can you make the event more attractive, or at what point should it be replaced by a new event?

Use these measurement characteristics (and others) to create your own event assessment form. Assign a weight factor (1, 2 or 3) to each characteristic depending on its importance. Assign a 1-to-5 rating to each characteristic (1=poor and 5=excellent). Multiply the score you have given each characteristic by the weight factor, then add each score to determine the event's overall assessment.

Content not available in this edition

Check Your Annual Event for Signs of Decline

For years, your nonprofit has staged the same annual fundraiser. But has your signature event lost its luster? How do you know when it is time to make changes to your event?

A key indicator of the health of your event is audience participation, says Samantha Swaim, who, as director/event strategist of Samantha Swaim Fundraising LLC, (Portland, OR), supports strategic planning for more than 20 fundraising events a year.

Asks Swaim, "Are folks eager to buy tickets or tables, or is your attendee list really declining? If this is the case, re-engage your audience by letting them in on the process and the planning. Folks will invest more if they feel a part of something."

Another major indication that your event is stalling, Swaim says, is that you are losing sponsors. To help prevent this, she advises keeping sponsors involved all year instead of just around the event. "Keep them engaged, make them feel a part of the organization's mission and keep them invested."

While falling profits can indicate your event is in trouble, the reason may have more to do with your fundraising goals than the event itself, says Judy Sitzer, owner of the New Philanthropy Group (Los Angeles, CA), an event planning agency that works strictly with nonprofits and stages galas and dinners for up to 1,600 people. "You have to be really realistic about how much money you think you can raise," says Sitzer. "Things go wrong when your expectations are unrealistic."

Sources: Judy Sitzer, Owner, New Philanthropy Group, Santa Monica, CA.
E-mail: judy@newphilanthropygroup.com
Samantha Swaim, Director/Event Strategist, Samantha Swaim Fundraising LLC, Portland, OR.
E-mail: sam@samanthaswaim.com

Restructure Your Struggling Fundraiser

If your fundraising event is suffering from decreased attendance and low revenues, take heart. A few simple fixes can revitalize it for years to come.

Samantha Swaim, director/event strategist of Samantha Swaim Fundraising LLC (Portland, OR), says you should evaluate your event to make sure it's a good fit for your audience, depending on their demographics. Consider these questions as you seek to redesign your event to best fit your audience:

1. Is it a group of friends that want time to socialize? Have you built in a social time for them?

2. Is your audience limited by schedule? Do you have a program that is tight and specific and makes good use of their time?

3. Does your crowd want the fun factor to be high and instead you've forced them into a long, slow program?

Next, Swaim says, look at the logistics to make sure your guests have a smooth experience. For example, "Do you have a good check-in and check-out system? Can guests easily get to the bars without a line? Do you have food when they're hungry and a seat when they're tired? A little investment in your logistics can keep things running smooth and improve the guests' overall impression of the event."

Finally, Swaim says, be sure that your program compels guests to make donations by establishing the importance of your cause.

"To increase your fundraising it is imperative that your guests know and understand the work that you do and feel a connection," Swaim says. "Use a video piece to take folks through the experience and impact of your organization." Avoid long speeches and keep programs short and simple.

If, after considering these factors, you still feel your event is in trouble, Swaim suggests taking an honest look at last year's event to determine what worked and what didn't. Keep the good parts and throw out everything else.

Source: Samantha Swaim, Director/Event Strategist, Samantha Swaim Fundraising LLC, Portland, OR.
E-mail: sam@samanthaswaim.com

Lightning Source UK Ltd.
Milton Keynes UK
UKOW06f2120020913

216389UK00008B/169/P